FIRST COMES LOVE

FIRST COMES LOVE

On Marriage and Other Ways of Being Together

TOM RASMUSSEN

BLOOMSBURY PUBLISHING
LONDON • OXFORD • NEW YORK • NEW DELHI • SYDNEY

BLOOMSBURY PUBLISHING
Bloomsbury Publishing Plc
50 Bedford Square, London, WC1B 3DP, UK
29 Earlsfort Terrace, Dublin 2, Ireland

BLOOMSBURY, BLOOMSBURY PUBLISHING and the Diana logo are
trademarks of Bloomsbury Publishing Plc

First published in Great Britain 2021

A catalogue record for this book is available from the British Library

ISBN: HB: 978-1-5266-2687-5; EBOOK: 978-1-5266-2686-8; EPDF: 978-1-5266-4532-6

2 4 6 8 10 9 7 5 3 1

Typeset by Newgen KnowledgeWorks Pvt. Ltd., Chennai, India
Printed and bound in Great Britain by CPI Group (UK) Ltd, Croydon CR0 4YY

To find out more about our authors and books visit www.bloomsbury.com
and sign up for our newsletters

For Shugs – who I would marry, if we believed in that sort of thing.

For Mum and Dad – whose marriage taught me to believe in that sort of thing.

Contents

Introduction: Every Second Someone in the World Gets Married

IT's A SUNDAY AFTERNOON in May, and it's excruciatingly hot on the Central Line. I'm offensively hungover, rolled in half on the tube after a very late night at a friend's wedding at which a group of us sat drinking neat vodka (why?), espousing the idiocy, the sheer lunacy, of marriage.

We're the guests people dread at their own weddings: the queers, the non-conformers, the eye-rollers, the critics, the bitchers, the moaners. I don't know why we're invited. And I don't know why we go.

We love our friends who got married: we love their love, and appreciate their right to marry, but we can't quite understand what the point of all this is.

As the sweat – which is mostly vodka – glides down my forehead and bounces off my eyebrows, I'm scrolling on my phone, connected to the omnipresent London underground Wi-Fi, and there I see it: 'Every second someone in the world gets married'.

It's a Compare the Market advert with the slogan that went viral when someone tweeted it captioned 'Poor Them'. It got thousands of retweets – and the responses were gruesome. Some celebrate the ad-libbed appraisal, others reject this Satan-worshipping cynicism in praise of the purity of O! Wonderful Sacred Marriage, some diagnose the Tweeter as lonely/sad/jealous/a loser. It seems everyone has an opinion on marriage – and it turns out, when I started asking my friends, family and random strangers in cafes (because that's what northerners do), everyone really does. Because, both historically and contemporarily, in western society it's expected of every single one of us. And if it's not then it's likely there's a good reason why. Ergo, opinions all round.

I get out at my stop and meet my friend who was also at the wedding last night, and we both dash for a pint to take the edge off the vodka distillery in our stomachs. We laugh, we talk about 'the normals' who get married, we joke about wedding fairs and anodyne idiots who spend thousands on their Big Day but are too strapped to give to homeless people.

And then my friend leaves, both of us feeling self-satisfied and cured of a hangover. Smug intellectual folk who have seen behind the curtain. But as I wave goodbye, my sense of satisfaction wanes. Because I've been lying.

The truth is, I'm desperate to get married, and I grew up obsessed with weddings. Obviously I haven't told anyone.

I haven't told anyone that all I want, really, is to slot into that statistic – to be another second in the ticking clock of weddings. I've always wanted it – I made a stunning, plump bride on the playground in primary school; I planned my offensively gay wedding to the letter throughout my teens; I wept over men who left me at university as the potential for marriage leaked out of my life; and I spent four years on a diet which I had joked to a friend was my Wedding Diet. We'd laughed, but I was deadly serious. I believed in marriage. I venerated it.

My parents had succeeded in staying together, where a lesser commitment could have seen them separated. Because in the north, where I'm from, when you get married you stay married. It's normal, it's safe. (Sadly, I don't have any divorce data by region in the UK because it's illegal to hack the YouGov website. But, having lived there for most of my life, I can tell you that it was either single-parent families from the off, or married couples who stayed together even when they hurled insults and pints of wine at each other.)

I craved the safety of wedlock more than my heterosexual siblings because I spent most of my childhood and adolescence feeling incredibly unsafe. Tormented, physically and emotionally, for being a basic white girl who loved weddings and who also happened to be in a boy's body. I grew up harbouring run-of-the-mill fixations: the shoebox filled with wedding trinkets, the obsession with romcoms, the memorisation of every single *Sex and the City* quote ever ('I'm getting married ... to myself, and I'm registered at Manolo Blahnik'), the Vera Wang couture dress. I was sure that when I met my groom he'd see me for me, and we would be wed, and I would curl up in his big lap and flick the remote as he pulled me in tight. I'd burn his Chicken Kiev in the oven but he would brush the hair away from my face and say, 'You're such a klutz,' – at this point I'd be giggling – 'it's what I love most about you, Rachel.' Obviously my name, in my head, was Rachel (probably Green, maybe McAdams à la *The Notebook*).

So, at twenty-two, I got engaged, in a field. I loved him, but I said yes all so that I could be a step closer to achieving the fantasy of matrimony. And I was electrified at the prospect: serotonin coursed through my body at the promise of legal and social security. No matter about the man, I would have the wedding.

Of course, like so many a lifelong promise made at the tender and drug-fogged age of twenty-two, that engagement crashed and burned, and then a lot changed in my life. I met a group of radical friends with iffy personal hygiene, I went on anarchist protests, I took my clothes off with six other people in Westminster in a bid to bring down Big Pharma (we never quite managed it), and I railed against The Man. Serotonin now began to flood through me at the thought of dismantling overbearing structures, not cementing them. See, to be part of a proper community of anarchic youths one must decry any and all pre-established structures: gender, sexuality, capitalism, marriage.

In working my way out of my life's ambition to be wed, I had connected my personal to the political, my political to the personal. Since that busted engagement I had railed too hard, too many times, against marriage and the patriarchal, homophobic structure from whence it came ever to consider getting married. I joined the anti-marriage camp, disappointing my poor mum in the process but impressing my friends and my vehemently anti-marriage now-boyfriend, Ace.

I text him from the pub, fuelled by the beer: Would you ever get married?

A reply.

No.

1

A Classy Wedding

WE GREW UP CONCERNED about money. Not the poorest of all the people we knew, but poor enough that Imperial Leather soap, at less than a pound per bar, was posh soap. In those years, when our family teetered at the drain of those affected by the late-noughties financial crash, it was marriage that kept my mum and dad together. Dad was moody, and Mum was stressed. But, like the smell of piss clings to the carpeted seats of the Bakerloo line, they had clung to each other.

And now here we all were in Edinburgh, in brighter financial times, over a decade since my dad's redundancy. Mum and Dad, able to look each other in the eye once more, wandered hand in hand around the hilly streets. We were about to attend what would surely be the wedding of the year: that of our close family friends, my long-time best mate Sam, to his long-time fiancée Abi. Sam and I had grown up very close – practically inseparable, and my mum and his mum were inseparable too. This was a family affair.

So when Sam met Abi, everyone was rather pleased that she had grown up in similarly hard times to us – in a family who undoubtedly, like mine and like Sam's, kept the Imperial Leather soap in a Ziploc bag under the sink, only to be excavated when guests came round. Whether, like mine, her grandma was iconic enough to have used the very same soap to brush her teeth with was unclear, but the bottom line was: we were all from families for whom there was a posh soap, a posh soap that denoted our desire not to appear poor to others.

Things were a little different now, however. Abi was head of a recruitment agency, after studying history at a Russell Group uni, and Sam was a banker in a big firm's Manchester office. They were upwardly mobile.

This wasn't your typical working-class wedding. That was my friend Anna's, who'd got married a year earlier at our local Catholic church and had the evening do at the nearby crumbling cricket club. It had been a perfect day – Iceland prawn rings and a traybake cake from ASDA with the couple's faces on it – and one which, if curated by a more middle-class London type, might have been the most hipster wedding imaginable. But this was not hipster. At one particularly poignant moment, Anna lost a shoe – only to discover it near-irrevocably glued to the sticky beer-stained carpet halfway across the room. Beautiful.

Sam and Abi's wedding was a wedding of class – a classy wedding – yet fitted perfectly to the tastes of the working classes. My family and I nearly wept when we heard how much they'd spent affirming their status as a couple done well: all to be played out, spent, celebrated over one single day. Sure, the pair had saved, for three years, in order to get married in the way they wanted. They'd made sacrifices, and while they'd end up spending more on their wedding than I have ever earned in one year, the cost of the celebration was still lower than the national average. Something Sam's mum was keen to remind us as she fluffed about our shared Edinburgh townhouse, red in the face from too much wine, too much spending.

While it seemed like a pricey affair, it wasn't overt, or grotesque, it was just lovely. Filled with lovely things loved by my increasingly distant best friend and his soon-to-be-wife. Yet as we clinked glasses and laughed at silly speeches, I thought about all the weddings I'd been to, all the money spent, all because we're told we should.

The difference between a working-class and a middle-class wedding is that the former must stand out, must compete as the Best of Them, as a pricey affair. The latter must be subtler, expensive in the right ways – distinguished caterers, sophisticated lighting, designer dress, all the signifiers of quality. Quality only recognised by those in the know. At a working-class wedding attendees must know how much has been spent, even if, as at my friend Anna's wedding, the kids' dessert is a single party ring biscuit.

A middle-class wedding, at least according to the array I've attended, will be more flippant about its own importance: it will prod fun at those who go all out, while speciously going all out. Middle-class people will laugh with a classist snarl at women who have tasteless princess weddings. Meanwhile, the middle-class bride will float around her parents' private woodland all day, beaming like a meek, newly wedded nymph. Middle-class people will be aware of the tropes and clichés of weddings, yet will fully engage with every tradition. 'Apparently there's a drag queen performing at the reception ... how different!' – a sentence I overheard at a very religious, middle-class wedding in Devon, at which I was performing. I was asked to sing Stevie Wonder's 'Isn't She Lovely'. A beautiful song, but hardly 'different'.

A list of middle-class weddings we've all been to:

- The wedding in the field where the bride has a muddy dress and an unappetising selection of finger food is presented on paper plates.
- The intimate occasion at the parental home in a wealthy London postcode, where it's just a few people because neither bride nor groom (assuming a heterosexual arrangement) really likes attention, or the idea of weddings, but both believe their love to be special enough to make this 'different'.
- The surprisingly Very Very Christian wedding of a couple who have never once mentioned God in your seven years of getting smashed together on weeknights.
- The fashion wedding where everything looks the same as the other fashion weddings on Pinterest, and the bride (assuming again that it's a heterosexual wedding, because aren't they all) will have chalky pink hair and the groom will have a beard and we will all drink craft beer and Veuve Clicquot and it will be expensive but it won't feel expensive. Hand-picked flowers.
- The wedding where there are far too many people and far too much purple lighting.
- The wedding where there's at least one famous actor in attendance, who does a turn in the middle of the reception (Jim Broadbent!).

- The wedding in the Cambridge college because wouldn't that be nice.

A working-class wedding must smack of achievement, because where I'm from it's the ultimate sign of success. This is a group of people who, not to generalise, work hard to avoid looking poor but will scream about a bargain so as not to be mistaken for a posh wanker. 'Love that top, Charlotte!' people might say to my mum. 'A pound! From George at Asda!' she'll reply. In Lancaster you can be ridiculed for having 'notions' – meaning 'ideas above your station'. Notions are something that I apparently had for wanting to, I dunno, move to London, or enjoy the expensive bit of the menu at the Frankie & Benny's next to the local Blockbuster. And yet nobody will think the bride who spends the equivalent of a house deposit on a wedding 'notional' whatsoever. See, where I'm from, marriage is a substitute for the graduation ceremony many people from places like my hometown will never have. Not into (arguably useless) academic excellence, in this case, but into adulthood. Into normality.

No matter how far one progresses in life, marriage is when a parent stops worrying, and when the world of my regional hometown stops thinking you're not normal. We ask questions about our 'strange' uncle who isn't married, with a tinge of pity. 'Poor Graham, he must be so lonely.' There's little airtime for the fact that he has a job he loves, or that he's much more sociable than most of the married units across the family. 'Maybe he's gay?' my late, brilliant grandma once asked me, false teeth jiggling at her gums. I agreed that perhaps he was, but also found it tragic that there was no other explanation for his being unmarried aged forty – he must be gay! I wonder whether my generation thinks differently about this, but it depends who you ask. If you were to ask my flatmates in London, for example, they'd all talk about how many over-forties they've bedded and move on. But if you were to ask my girlfriends from school, all of whom are married, planning their weddings, or forcing their passive boyfriends to pop the question on a hot-air balloon ride they've bought their other halves as a gift, they would think it was odd – sad, not normal – not to be married by your early thirties.

Then there's the strange marrieds: the pair who actually are gay, the pair who never spend a night in the same bed, the pair who are more like friends than partners. And while everyone has marital problems, we judge these people with alacrity.

'They should get divorced then!' my mum, who knows far better than that, will conclude. 'But they're happy, Mum, and they stayed together for the kids/it works for them/ maybe companionship is enough,' I'll reply. But my mum won't listen. I love her for the sometimes absurd opinions she holds, which she knows are ill-informed – a classic northern matriarchal trait. But if it doesn't fit the preset category of marriage, then a marriage is improper, dark and, yes, strange to people from my hometown, the same people who've despised the sight of their partners from day two of the honeymoon. Isn't everyone a Strange Married?

The Strange Marrieds' very decision to marry way back when was inflicted upon them by the people who judge them for their dynamic now – those who stand at the local pub, still smoking inside, jibing at any and all difference while being, ironically, the most wonderfully eccentric people you could imagine. Everyone here was born, raised and stayed in a place where being unmarried would result in nothing short of social-pariah status. And so some people found life rafts, or beards, in each other, and they grew together into a glistening, complicated, fluid arrangement that suits both partners. Like my old friend Harriet's parents – her mum was gay, her dad was fine with it (until she left him for a woman she'd met at the gym); or like my friend Becky's parents who had been separated for years but put on such a good show that nobody, not even the kids, found out until the youngest one had turned eighteen. And when the cracks in these relationships appear, people judge in the same way they would judge should these couples have remained single instead. Perhaps people feel distaste for these strange marital set-ups because they are subverting the ordinary from within, asking questions that others are unwilling to answer about their own arrangements.

In her book *Public Vows: A History of Marriage and the Nation*, historian Nancy Cott describes marriage in medieval Europe as an institution that 'prescribes duties and dispenses privileges', but how different are things now? Marriage remains a tool of the state: a way of keeping society in a recognisable shape. The state depends on the union of two people to produce something that in turn contributes to its purpose: children, assets, debts – all things that are managed by married couples so that a civil society (as we know it) can function in a methodical, controlled way and the state won't be stuck with the difficulty of raising abandoned kids or supporting ex-spouses or, god forbid, caring for ailing singletons. Divide – into pairs – and conquer.

I wonder why these unusual arrangements create such discomfort among the married folk of my hometown, and I reason that it's because watching people manipulate an institution you have believed in your whole life forces you to ask questions you were never allowed to pose. If people can do the normal thing but differently, then maybe everything you believe in becomes fallible. And so instead of leaning closer to the truth, we criticise those at the un-smooth edges of marriage and normality.

This causes me to hesitate coming to my mum, or those in my family who worship at the altar of marriage, with my critiques of it. I wonder, when they pass judgement on those in alternative set-ups, if I could ever tell them that I want an open marriage, or a polyamorous marriage, or even a gay marriage to my partner whom my family loves so much (except for my rabidly homophobic cousin Joy, but she won't be getting a 'save the date' anytime soon either way). I wonder if my mum would ever understand if I choose not to get married. Perhaps that's doing her a disservice; she's actually wildly accepting and probably wouldn't give a shit. She'd still call me ridiculous, though. But we'd be laughing and I'd say it right back at her.

Sam and Abi had worked very hard to ensure their wedding would be one for the books. Now, this strongly suggests that the purpose of the day, of the spending, was actively performative. It wasn't: just like me, Sam enjoyed luxuries that would have been considered absurd when we were growing up. And, much like most weddings, it was still an event focused largely on status – one that would show the pair's many (well-deserved) adorers just how much they could spend. It would remind those less cultured that Abi, being a lover of history, knew the caverns of this castle well: its history, its romance. It would remind those less financially well-endowed (namely everyone except

Sam's banker friends) that Sam earned a good salary. None of this is intentional or malicious, of course, it's just the cultural code we are all ensnared in: capitalism. It's the same reason I buy Raf Simons coats – so people will know I've made a success of myself, even if I don't have (and I'm not exaggerating) a hundred pounds left in my account. It's the reason people practically bankrupt themselves when planning and executing their weddings. Unless you're using 'daddy's plastic' – a line someone at uni once used while paying for a cocktail on a thick, platinum credit card.

Every detail was perfect: from the groom's tailor-made suit to the very *The Lost JFK Tapes* Ray-Bans he wore the whole week (even though it rained the entire time); from the gaudy fireworks display and the feast of fresh fish and grilled meats, to the bride's veil that drifted breezily through every picture, taken, incidentally, by a photographer who had recently shot for Chanel. I wondered about the limoncello I was drinking, and aperitifs in general. Did anyone actually like them, or do we feel simply as though we should, because if you do like them – much like *Fleabag*, or long walks, or the Tate Britain – you come across as cultured, as worldly, as open-minded? And this seemed, in part, the point of Sam and Abi's fancy wedding. It was an opportunity to cement their reputations as people on the ascent – far from my mum and dad, or Sam's mum and dad, who married in a registry office, or my mate Anna who served, I shit you not, a Wotsit atop a cheese single atop half a barm cake at her wedding breakfast (it was delicious).

My family, and Sam's too, while they might not expressly say this, are pretty socialist: critical of the way wealth is distributed, huge believers in the NHS and nationalisation, and long-time haters of Maggie Thatcher. But this was not a socialist wedding (unsure what a socialist wedding would look like, tbh). And yet, unquestioningly, we celebrated every choice made by Sam and Abi, who both suffer from the same condition I do: wanting, even if we are ashamed to admit it, to be a little bit middle class. Of course, we hated Thatcher too and loved the NHS, but our paths had arguably led us more to the liberal left even if it hurts to say it. Not a peep came from my parents or Sam's increasingly stressed mother – before, during or after the wedding – about the money spent. They were up dancing and drinking in the view and the free-flowing champagne. And for a night we were all posh. And for a night it was wonderful. But why, when it comes to weddings, do they cast a kind of amnesiac spell over people and their politics?

Historically, marriage was drawn along class lines. Poor people could marry poor people, and rich people would be traded like pawns in a giant aristocratic chess game ordered by land, assets and national interest. Sam and Abi weren't bucking any historic trend: they were two peasants getting married, only now under advanced-stage capitalism they did have assets – all of which they shared ahead of signing on the dotted line and exchanging rings.

I was best man. A complicated role for someone who, for some time, hasn't identified with the category of man. I am proudly non-binary, and proudly supported by my family, even though they get my pronoun wrong 80 per cent of the time. We had toyed with the title 'Best Queen' or 'Best Person' but for some reason it didn't really stick. That's not on Sam – he would have proudly had me officiate in full drag if I wanted to – but I was confused at how uncomfortable I felt, I feel, at weddings when I have to jigsaw my gender into proceedings. Any solution fails: Best Man and I'm misgendered, Best Queen and I stick out like a sore thumb. It's nobody's, or perhaps everybody's, fault that when it comes to weddings there's a prevailing feeling that This Is Not For You. Instead, I would force myself, through a blindingly dysphoric head-spin, to wear a suit and be addressed by all as a best man. My gender, or my critique of it, was temporarily deleted, the years of work it had taken to reach this point vanishing swiftly as I googled how to knot a tie – something I hadn't done since high school. There was to be no conversation about anything alternative: this was to be a nice day, a lovely day, a normal day. And I was in on it, I would happily follow suit.

The tragic implications of these subliminal commands from myself and others (which occur at every wedding ever) while not outright violent, incite a more subtle form of pain – one invisible to the naked eye, but blinding to those of us who have borne these microaggressions forever. The basic implication is that anything that you are is not nice, not lovely, not normal. My gender isn't nice, lovely, normal. My lifestyle isn't nice, lovely, normal. Simple words gain the power to momentarily tie you into knots more complicated than the Windsor I had to ask my dad to do for me in the end. And really, much of this is a feeling as opposed to a reality, with nobody in attendance at Sam's wedding being anything but celebratory about who I am, and what I do when I'm not wearing a suit.

Of course it's not this suit-shaped single microaggression that causes so much hurt; we're not so weak that we can't withstand the odd mistake or miscommunication. It's an accumulation of these words and emotions over a number of years spent tugging uncomfortably in the confines of normalcy, especially on occasions when your very presence threatens the foundation of the thing you're supposed to be celebrating. There's a public/private aspect to acceptance; it's one rule among close units, but infinitely more complicated, fraught, when it's an 'event' that involves the wider family, family friends, or the rest of the world. I'd experienced similar feelings at christenings, birthdays, awards ceremonies, congratulatory meals for my brother who had just been promoted at work; I'd had that feeling at funerals, graduations, community events. Always that I should be the one to tone it down – whatever 'it' means – to allow others to feel comfortable. I'm very happy for people to feel comfortable, but not at the expense of others and not if that comfort means welcoming subtle or not-so-subtle dynamics of intolerance. When my dad's friend casually used a racist slur at a family meal, it was my challenging of it that was penalised: I had made things awkward for everyone else. Why did the racist comment not merit the same? Both my parents agreed with me, even if they didn't say anything at the time. This logic, a tyranny of 'normalcy', seems to prevail necessarily at weddings. Is that really where we want to be today?

It's moments like these – where I'm forced through the choices of others to conceal my own (although my gender identity, arguably, isn't a choice) – that I feel allergic both to the idea of weddings, and my participation in upholding these traditions. The feeling of concealment, of 'not making a scene', is ever-present in many gender non-conforming people's lives. It is amplified at weddings where binaries are cemented for no other reason than tradition. And if this is the basis of acceptable weddings, how could a non-man with a man's body ever marry a man?

When did Sam make the choice to be cis, I wondered, as he strolled gallantly down the aisle, his big arms from his lifelong gym obsession wrapped around his new bride's tiny waist. Their physicality was the perfect metaphor for the circus of marriage as I most fear it – the strong man and the disappearing woman.

Abi is an avid feminist, a lover of Mary Beard, an intelligent woman who prides herself on her bookish smarts – she wouldn't go down silently as is expected of so many brides on their wedding days, and she certainly wouldn't be disappearing. Some hours later, as the sun set over Calton Hill, she gave a speech inciting Countless Strong Women From History. She stood up, to genuine audible gasps from onlookers in shock at the rupturing of the tradition of the silent bride, and spoke about Being A Powerful Woman – in a wedding gown, on a terrace, next to a giant war cannon, having just committed herself into a structure historically designed to trade her, to oppress her, to own her (a part of history which she, of course, left out of her speech).

A beautiful scene. A strange scene. Here was an intelligent couple, both forward-thinking, left wing, fairly good allies to marginalised people: we'd had long red wine-fuelled dinners where we discussed the nuances of cis privilege and the hetero-patriarchy – and time after time all three of us would come down on the same side, sure in the knowledge that these systems were both oppressive and inauthentic to the realities of day-to-day living, even for a heterosexual couple. Abi could name countless examples where her energies and actions were more masculine than Sam's who, despite his hench appearance, once cried when I told him Buffy died at the end of season five (sorry, spoiler, but if you haven't watched it at this point then shame on you). Sam was aware of this fact too, and relished the idea that he might be the living example of what a male feminist could look like; in more recent years, he had gone about co-founding his work's LGBT society to learn how to become a better ally.

So it was baffling to me that on this day, on any wedding day for that matter, the main priority is tradition. At weddings, there's no space for conversation or criticism – it's a day meant for happiness, for celebrating man and wife – a painful phrase – and for not bringing gender or class or anything divisive to the table.

On this day where everyone should be at their happiest, it confused me that instead of doing the things that made us actually happy – like debating politics and railing against oppressive structures and behaviours, all while getting smashed and eating kebabs messily – we sang along to the happy couple's first dance and laughed audibly as Abi shoved a wedge of rustically iced three-tiered cake into Sam's mouth as if this was what happiness looked like. And they were happy, of course they were, and we were happy for them. But why does a formal celebration of that happiness often cleave off the messiest, happiest parts? Like my one friend who loves a drink more than almost anything decided that, at her wedding, she shouldn't drink at all. Or my other friend who hadn't been to church in years, yet got married in the most solemn Catholic ceremony I've ever witnessed.

I found myself down a whirlpool, saying things I absolutely didn't agree with. 'Haven't they done well?' I rejoiced to the mother of the bride. Done well: what does that even mean?

So there I was, burning alive in a suit both because of the heat and my deep hatred for what it represented. I was feeling angry and proud, disappointed at having to meet someone else's idea of normal, and moved to tears at Sam and Abi's love, that they had got what they wanted. No one deserved happiness more than Sam: the man who stuck up for me on the schoolyard, the first person I ever told I was gay.

I spent the following morning on my own walking around Edinburgh before the whole family, my boyfriend included, was set to join a wedding-party walk (hell) up Arthur's Seat. I watched as people ate breakfast and spent money at tartan-tourist stalls down cobbled alleyways, and I felt like we'd all come so far from who we were. Sam had certainly arrived at the expected in one way – the heterosexual, married way. Now it was the day after the wedding and it had been a huge, stunning, memorable success, even though the bride and groom's families had spent so much they would later stand at the cashpoint on the Royal Mile flinching as they each withdrew £75 for an evening meal. Sam had gone down a road less travelled, as I had, but where affluence was the badge of his new identity, queerness was mine.

Of all of my family and friends, I've perhaps travelled furthest away from where I grew up – both geographically and ideologically. I've gone down the road, over the hill, through the whitewater rapids, and fallen off the cliff less travelled, so to speak. Mine and Sam's parents had worked their whole lives to survive, with kids who, relative to some of the people we knew growing up, never wanted for anything. This didn't mean we had a pool and two holidays abroad a year. It meant there was always food, heating, hobbies, birthday and Christmas presents and money for a takeaway on a Friday. Through their hard work, they created opportunity for their children to self-actualise: it's because of them I don't have to be a carer like my mum was at my age and can instead make a full-time living from drag, writing and singing. Not many people who grew up like me get to do that.

I spent my twenties doing what Sam and Abi didn't – and proudly. Sure, until the age of twenty, like Sam I'd sought normality: I studied for a veterinary medicine degree, searched desperately for a husband and, one winter, even wore a gilet with no irony whatsoever. And by the age of twenty-two I was engaged. Jackpot. It was the speediest way of securing a kind of social safety that had never been afforded a young, fat, working-class, femme-gay person. The kind of social safety I never saw Sam have to fight for. The world hadn't really loved me, but my then fiancée did – and so I'd said yes. But when that engagement fell apart, I felt normality had failed me a final time, and so I dove head first into my rejection of it.

I moved into a squat with some brilliant queers who prioritised anything above normality. Stuff like wanking together and spray-painting our washing machine gold, though we never got round to plugging it in. These were people who wanted something big – something else – and so did I. With them I took drugs, I got kicked out of Berghain for passing out in the middle of an orgy after taking too much ecstasy. I bounced around town, in heels, dresses, wigs, make-up, in Ubers as the sun came up or on Boris bikes in a fringe dress that tangled in the spokes, irresponsibly and wonderfully desperate to keep! the! party! going! I became a drag queen and chose to be broke rather than to work a job that rolled ahead of me for the rest of my life. Plus, I got fired from my first café job because, while they never said as much, I think I got caught on camera getting bum-fingered behind the bar. (Good times.) I laughed in the face of normality – family, car, kids, marriage, nine-to-fives, having savings, a planned-out future – determined instead to play out the wildest scenario in order to affirm my status as queer, as non-conforming, as someone who didn't want what everyone else wanted me to want.

I cackled with friends around dinner tables at how boring marriage is, and made vows to queer girls that we'd live in communes and raise each other's babies. I took city break after city break, determined to do anything but save because there'd be, thankfully, no wedding for me, no baby for me, no spouse to support, no mortgage to pay. I slept with over a hundred people in three years, of whom I can recall perhaps five names (a good thing, frankly). I would be non-binary and nomadic – I would live my label and free myself from the boring mill of the everyday by choosing the most fabulous option, always. Between the years 2014 and 2017 I ate every single meal in a restaurant, and refused to cook at home, even if it meant draining my overdraft and eating alone.

On reflection, wilfully making abnormal choices doesn't make you not-normal – and as glittering and wondrous as those years were they screamed of a performativity, the same way Sam and Abi's wedding did. All this time I was leaning into another kind of expectation and after four years of performed wildness it hit me on my twenty-sixth birthday that I didn't know if I could continue to live like this. Exhausted, broke, constantly serotonin-deficient. A wedding? No, I didn't want that. But a four-year comedown wasn't pushing my buttons either. There I was, with no stability, no money, no real job, a collection of wigs and a murder of scars on my liver. I deify those who continue to live life in this way, I think it's remarkable and brave and glorious and political. It's something I yearn for ideologically, but I wonder whether in reality I am perhaps too 'normal' after all, or simply don't have the stamina?

This idea of normal has moved incrementally over all these hazy years. When I left Lancaster I wanted what I considered, back then, to be normal. What Sam and Abi had just achieved. Marriage, children. I was going to be a large animal vet, and nobody would know I was gay (who was I kidding) except my stay-at-home husband and my gorgeous 2.4 children. Then I quit – a mix of classism, acrylic nails and a nervous breakdown brought into focus the crashing realisation that I would never be happy with a career that is 65 per cent euthanising animals – and moved to that squat, which we'll lovingly name Wally Lodge from hereon – with little money but a deep, hot want for experiences. At first the things I did shocked me: the wild sex, the late nights and lost days, the ease with which I swallowed all the drugs even though I'd been vehemently anti-drugs since I first learned that you could drown by drinking too much water when you're on ecstasy. And much like that ecstasy urban legend, my desire for normality washed away with each sip of water. Or perhaps my idea of normal just changed. Normal for me is actually a room full of semi-naked queer people fucking; normal for me is brightly coloured hair; normal for me is my flatmates and me masturbating together for fun.

Repositioning, or finding this 'new normal', wasn't an inherently easy thing to do. Drugs, dicks and drag weren't even peripherally in view as I grew up, and yet the moment I found queerness – not totally unlike the moment Abi and Sam found each other – I committed to it and made choices that would telegraph that thing about me to the world. I looked the other way; I decided that my deeply normative desires were like oil on the water of my new life, immiscible and incompatible.

It's only with the gift of hindsight that you can collect all your snap decisions into a pattern. Sam and Abi, for instance, earned more then spent more; Sam bought a watch, worked more, earned more, then bought a more expensive watch. And he liked how that felt, evidently. He's told me that before. I am the same with my queerness. I would suck a dick in an alleyway, my friends would tell me I'm queer; so I'd fuck twelve guys in a night and my friends would tell me I'm more queer. Yes, my choices were perhaps more radical and less socially acceptable than Sam and Abi's, but I was still engaging in status play the way they did with their wedding in the hallowed halls of Edinburgh Castle. In chasing non-conformity I think perhaps I've been sucked into another set of rules that also wallpaper over my most authentic desires. Queerness, for sure. But also a similar kind of capitalist acquisition structure: acquire more queer experience, have more queer capital. Obviously this isn't me exalting the joys of normality. Please! It's just that I don't quite know what it is I want.

And so there's something here, inside my head, or beneath that wallpaper, that I can't quite locate. After flitting swiftly between deep desire and harsh critique, I find myself now somewhere in the middle, realising that when it comes to marriage, not everything is clear-cut. Nothing is singular, nothing exists in a vacuum, and ideology and reality are often incompatible. My ideology tells me to be as queer as possible but my body and reality tell me I need an early night. My mind tells me I think marriage is for losers, for the normies, for people who aren't very free-thinking. But my body, my heart, the way I feel when I think about marrying my partner, Ace, tell me that that's what I want. I can no longer pretend that my ideological position reflects my feelings, much as I have tried. Not unlike capitalism, or that time I had green hair – some things work in theory, but are untenable in practice.

The naivety of extreme youth wears off after a while. Before, I was fearless, harsh, principled. Now, since that fearlessness saw me hospitalised and my principles had been challenged and proven wrong on endless occasions, I don't know what's what. I don't know what I think about marriage, and I don't know why, but I know that I think I want it.

Sat there at the top of Arthur's Seat as the late afternoon sun pierced the heavy Scottish clouds, I looked at Ace. I felt an overwhelming desperation, bursting at my ribcage, to ask for his hand in marriage. When I look at him, here at this love-soaked wedding, I think that he's the person I want to look after in sickness and in health; he's the person I want to choose curtains with, and learn to cook roast dinners with; the person I want to pick up stuff from the shop for, on my way home after a long day at work, even though he's had a day off; the person whose washing I want to do if it will make his life even a fraction easier. I want our things to be merged and I want to buy him things I can't afford and I want to go to places with him and watch him smile as he sees something new for the first time. I want to make him feel as safe as he makes me feel, because we've both spent a lot of our lives walking down the street when it's dark out, feeling our heart rates quicken because we're visibly queer and you never quite know if tonight will be the night when someone chooses to take their pain out on you. I want to stay in on a Saturday night with him and watch reruns of TV shows we've seen countless times and not for a second feel like I'm wasting my life because time spent with him is never time wasted. I want to see him laugh, and I want to have weeks where we don't know if we'll get through it but we do. I want to be so naive and trusting that I believe we can do it, forever, when, in reality, forever doesn't exist. But why is it that these desires all lead to the punchline of a proposal? Why does wanting these things feel so inextricably tied to wanting to wear a ring?

It's not as though all marriages are built on a bedrock of care, and certainly having the ring on the finger doesn't mean any of the things I want with Ace are more guaranteed than they were before we'd descend into an unsound institution. Plus, it's likely a useless battle here because Ace is from the sort of brilliant middle-class family who could easily slot into a Four Weddings-type movie, each of them representing the staunchly anti-marriage folk at the reception.

It's a shame that I'm becoming more normal really. I'd hoped that after fifteen years of being out, queer, gay, stripping back expectations, stripping away friends and family members and certain opportunities and ways of life, to get to the core of who I actually am, that I would have an answer to life's big questions. But, like clockwork, the panic has set in and time has turned a proud nihilist into someone who seeks safety above all things. Since I was attacked on the street in drag some years ago, I have found it more satisfying to blend in, to keep my once-ostentatious protest against the norm behind closed doors, to choose safety. Perhaps this is why I'm craving marriage after all: the social security it offers, with a partner who makes me feel as safe as Ace does is enough. There's nothing to lose, bar the approval of some of my old clubbing friends, though a wedding will be a chance for them to get high, so I'm sure they won't mind too much.

We spent the final day in Edinburgh at the house. We ate tomatoes and bread for our final meal and watched *Four Weddings*, because we'd spent too much to go out.

2

Not All Marriage Is Created Equal

Love Is Love is perhaps the most inane sentiment ever
uttered. Love Wins, a close second.

These two phrases – the gay equivalent of the straight
and much worse Live, Laugh, Love – were, and continue
to be, synonymous with a certain kind of LGBTQIA+
equality. The kind that gets chucked about at corporate
dinners, plastered on HMRC's Twitter account
throughout the month of June, and slapped across a tub
of Itsu noodles every Pride. The problem isn't that these
phrases are offensive (don't worry, I'm not that sensitive).
The problem is that they aren't offensive enough.

Now, one can't write them off entirely because part of
a move towards equality for those who are oppressed is
making our message digestible to the most basic people

imaginable (the government, bigoted heterosexuals, popular posh podcasters). And so Love is Love and Love Wins were, and are, gently useful tools; a non-threatening way of saying 'give us our fucking rights you bigoted fucking fucks and then watch us laugh while you burn.' I guess #giveusourfuckingrightsyoubigotedfuckingfucksthenwatchuslaughwhileyouburn has less of a ring to it.

They're also subtly manipulative statements when applied to faggotry and fag marriage: if I say Love Is Love and apply to it to us gays, and our right to wed, and you then disagree, you're automatically exposing yourself as a homophobe, as someone who doesn't believe that Gay/Queer/Bi/Pan/Trans Love Is Actual Love. And since people are often far more concerned with not appearing bigoted, than, y'know, actually not being bigoted, these catchphrases become easy to regurgitate. Like a bird mother sicking up easily digestible food into her young's mouth: but in this case it's an influencer who does sponcon with Boohoo dot com, posting a floral graphic that reads Love is Love to their stories. These statements are clever because they co-opt people into support of the LGBTQIA+ community, without them having to get their feeds/minds/mouths dirty. And so these simple catchphrases which cut nowhere near to the heart of the fight for gay marriage, or other far more vital forms of LGBTQIA+ equality, become semi-useful tools with which to win over apolitical people into buying into the nice clean queer message.

Don't worry, this is not the hill upon which I am going to die for this chapter. Messaging is important, optics can be helpful. But frankly I don't really care what Urban Outfitters prints on a crop top just in time for Pride every year. What I do care about is queer love. And that is a hill upon which I will happily die.

The issue with these phrases is that they do not work hard enough to detail the miracle of queer love. The superiority of queer love. I wish I could tell you in words how it felt to receive news of my two queer friends getting married next month, knowing that for innumerable people before us such a public display would have been both impossible and, at certain times in history, or in certain places around the world presently, punishable by death or imprisonment. I wish I could tell you in words what queer love really feels like, when you have grown up knowing that every single person around you thinks that the queer love that you desire or experience is not love. Is not normal. But if I were to try to tell you in words, I would end up writing something as flimsy as Love is Love.

Why? Because our love has had/will always have boundaries to break. Dominant love, white heterosexual middle-class thin able-bodied love rarely, if ever, did. Gay love is miraculous. Queer love is miraculous. Trans love, dyke love, lesbian love, asexual love, bisexual love, aromantic love, cross-orientation love. It's miraculous. It's more than love.

And it doesn't just win. It overcomes. It pushes back against years of violence, histories of oppression, presents of murder and misunderstanding and powerful men in positions they don't deserve constantly reminding us just how fragile our rights are. In Poland, as I write, the prime minister is leading his electoral campaign with a promise to ban gay marriage; in the UK conversion therapy is up for debate and the Gender Recognition Act looks like it won't receive the reform it so desperately needs despite overwhelming public support; in the USA, 2020 was the most deadly year on record for black trans women, while Trump revealed new threats to our rights daily and gave briefings on how to 'spot' a trans woman. It doesn't bear naming the number of countries who criminalise homosexuality since the British imported their homophobic colonial-era laws to other people's homelands. Us queers live within an intricate, long-constructed nexus of local, national and international violence, and have done for centuries, and yet our Love Still Wins; our Love Has Always Been Love.

It was love in the molly houses of the 1700s where gays would meet behind whitewashed windows. Love won in the Gateways club in Chelsea in the 1940s and '50s, a place for clandestine lesbian meet-ups. It thrived in quieter spaces, like in the 365 letters exchanged between Benjamin Britten and Peter Pears, or the likely thousands of other queer love letters written by people who weren't famous composers or their singing muses. It blossomed into secret languages like Polari, Gayle, green carnations or the hanky code. It hid secretly, yet in plain sight, in the countless marriages between women in the 1500s, where one woman would commit so readily to her wife that she would dress, from thereon, in man's clothing and trick a priest into endorsing a religiously recognised marriage. And it continues to find light in places where it's criminalised.

And it is love between Ace and me. It is love when we're in Paris, eating at Café Charlot, looking at each other and sitting in silence again. It is love when I tell him he's the only person I know who I think is going to heaven even though we both know heaven likely doesn't exist. He looks at me and I know that he thinks that if there was a heaven he wouldn't want to go unless I went with him. And I think that maybe this is heaven, and maybe he does too.

But then the bill comes and we remember it's not heaven because in heaven capitalism is abolished, and marriage most probably is too, as is monogamy because jealousy and fear obviously doesn't exist there.

But it was still love when, the next day, it was non-binary awareness day and that morning I'd been tagged seven times in different online posts about non-binary people worth following and I'd also been talked about in an article in the *Spectator* by some journalist who referred to me as someone who was harming children (because I contributed to a podcast for kids on the BBC where I simply explained the term queer in a discussion on identity). And I was feeling sad about both of those things. I was feeling sad that my existence couldn't just be non-politicised, non-dramatic, non-worth-following, non-read-as-perverse-because-I-want-to-give-kids-like-me-something-I-didn't-have. And then we walked out of the flat to get lunch and I told Ace how I was feeling. And he just listened quietly. And then Shola Ama's 'You Might Need Somebody' came on in the brasserie, and I said 'I love this song it's Shola Ama's "You Might Need Somebody"' and he clutched his heart and told me he loves me so much, that he loves it when I know the names of songs and artists he would never know the names of. And it's in this texture that I'm reminded he loves me in so many ways nobody else can: not because I'm non-binary, or named in an article as someone to follow, or because he needs to defend me from TERFs disguised as journalists. But because none of those things matter to how he sees me, and loves me, and wants me. And here we were again, that feeling of wanting to propose bursting from my ribs, and thinking that there was no way in words to express it. That beyond the things I have named myself as, someone loves the white noise in between my seven identity labels, because that's where I really am.

And I feel, yet again, a rising need to ask him if he'll marry me because – as I don't have the words to explain what this feeling feels like – I don't have the societal marker to show him, to show anyone else, either.

Marriage feels like the only way to show someone just how seriously you feel about them, to show them just how many times they've saved you. And as the feeling rises again, bubbling up as I swallow my French onion soup, I stifle it – catch it in my mouth and gulp it back down just like that gooey oniony goodness.

The move to grant homosexual marriage was something that had been fought for long and hard, and Love Won and Love Was Love, and our love – for the first time in a long time – was granted the same right as anyone else's. Gays got married, and conservatives fought against it, and gays still got married. And for a moment our love was let into the idea of normality: something so many of us have had lasting, complicated relationships with.

When the fight died down, and the politicians across the USA tweeted #LoveWins, and David Fucking Cameron was awarded LGBTQIA+ ally of the year at the PinkNews Awards, many queer people were left reeling with unanswerable questions about what this new and important inclusion into normality meant for us. Our communities had suffered painfully at the hands of our legal exclusion from state unions and those sanctioned by religion. But now we were set free by governmental gatekeepers. Or were we?

Obviously not.

Because being barred from the most historic, most ubiquitous global institution created a centuries-long cultural belief that our Love Is Inherently Not Love. In turn, this created centuries' worth of fractured families – parents and siblings, aunties and uncles – who, at worst, kick you out of the house because your love can't fit into their understanding, or, at best, feel a deep sense of disappointment that their child will never be normal. Never be the way they planned. This cultural belief echoes out into schoolyards, classrooms, books, films and, perhaps most distressingly, deep into the psyches of countless queer people who grew up with the knowledge that they could never be normal. That they could never do their parents proud. That their Love Couldn't Win.

My community, a teeny-tiny 5–10 per cent of the population, ended up with, proportional to our size, the highest suicide rates of any in the west; same for alcoholism; same for homelessness; same for depression, anxiety, drug dependency. Members of my community die younger – either at the hands of others, themselves, or the permanently heightened amounts of cortisol in our bloodstream because of a constant fear of violence and misunderstanding, which leads to literal heart attack.

It might be over-egging the importance of marriage to say that our exclusion from it directly produced all of these realities. But marriage is the pinnacle of western culture's understanding of love, of how we express it, and it's the most common organisational structure for many people's lives. So our exclusion from it, it might be argued, was something that compounded the ways in which people misunderstood us, and misunderstood our love. If the Great Institution of Marriage didn't deem us worthy, then perhaps we were not.

But much like those in the molly houses, or the women who tricked the Church into marrying them, much like those who spoke Polari and cruised on the Heath, our community created a culture of love away from the prying eyes of normality. We cultivated new ways to love, new family structures, new identities – or old ones set free. We told each other we were worthy. And our love was, is, more than love. It was resistance, it was power, it was radical.

And then equal marriage was allowed, and we were given the right to acculturate our powerful, radical, resistive love into the singular option presented to us by society: marriage. Normality.

It's an attractive option. It's like finally being accepted by the popular girls at school who used to bully you all the livelong day.

But do we really want to be friends with the bullies? Do we really want the same rights as everyone else? And do we really need them? Does giving us what the oppressive classes already have really liberate us? Many queer activisms of the past didn't think equal marriage would solve the inequalities under which our communities suffered. Certainly the demands of queer activism in the 1970s were not marriage-focused: in fact many of the loudest voices in the movements seeking our liberation saw marriage as a worthless bargaining chip, something which would not only not suffice, but might also serve to create a problematic intercommunity dynamic between the ideal, assimilated homosexuals and the scrappy, ruffian unmarried queers. As Colin Ashley wrote in the New Labour Forum in 2015, 'the campaign for marriage equality assumes a monolithic LGBT/Q political constituency and has ignored the internal segmentations that produce starkly unequal rights within the LGBT/Q population.' The Gay Liberation Front's 1971 manifesto actively critiqued marriage as something intrinsically linked to racism, classism, misogyny, transphobia and homophobia, and the LGBT(QIA+) causes at the time were unified under the idea that current systems as we know them – in this case, marriage especially – must be abolished if the most marginalised in our communities were ever to be truly uplifted.

Why then, when I care more about the most marginalised in my community than I do about normality, do I feel a pull towards this idea of marriage so many of my forebears denounced? Perhaps I'm seeking more protection, bearing in mind that I've never held Ace's hand in public, in London, or Lancaster, or Paris. But a marriage certificate won't solve that.

The weekend after the first gay marriage happened in the UK – 29 March 2014 – my friends and I were out clubbing in east London. As with any good night out, it ended with me being spit-roasted by two older men in a gay sauna in Vauxhall. One of these men, the one who spent most of his time at the front, had a wedding ring on: and I asked him, after he'd finished on my face, if he was married. 'Kind of,' he answered, wiping himself down, probably feeling the same heady jitters of pleasure and shame I always feel when I've just climaxed with a complete stranger on a bench under buzzing red lights. 'But we're planning to do it properly now.'

I congratulated him keenly, and then he walked out of the cubicle and back into a sea of naked, shivering men. I remember, in that moment alone, feeling awash with absolute joy that this man was able to plan a brand-new future with his partner, one that queers like us had never been afforded before. One that, being at least double my age, he would never have dreamed of being a possibility until recently.

As I got dressed I thought more about how this legislation had been passed a year ago and how that was, is, far too late. How so much damage had already been done. And as I left and waited for the night bus home, I wondered what this man felt. If he felt excited, or that his time had been wasted. If he felt disappointed that his evidently non-normative way of loving was being boxed into something as small and as limited as marriage. None of us know the long-term effect this inclusion will have upon our community.

Don't get me wrong, it's important we secured these rights. The more the better. And while many marriage cynics, myself included, bemoan the patriarchal institution and its prioritisation of monogamy in place of sexual freedom – the latter being something many LGBTQIA+ activists have decreed one of our most important tools in the fight for queer liberation – it's important to remember that not every queer person is an activist, and not every queer person is armed with the education, culture, social capital, geographical proximity or context to free themselves from the chains of structural demands such as marriage. Even if they do have access to those things, they might not want to. We have to ask ourselves the question: does a queer person's happiness matter more to me than whether or not they agree with my stance on marriage? The answer should be yes, otherwise your radical activism is dislocated.

For Jack, an ex-heterosexual-bully-turned-gay-friend from my hometown, marriage is something he absolutely aspires to; it's something he believes will bring him happiness. 'Well my sister got married. I wanna get married.' He tells me over Instagram message that he's too busy to chat on the phone because he's a canteen assistant at the hospital near where we grew up, and he's between night shifts. 'I dunno, am not arsed for shagging about and stuff, I want a house and stuff and a man who loves me. A strong one for some protection and that.'

Do you think people would take your gayness more seriously, up in Lancaster, if you got married? I ask. 'Dunno. I guess it's important for my mum and stuff, and for me and my family, and I reckon it would be a nice way to show everyone what was worried about me being gay that they don't have to be. That I can be normal like everyone else.'

Would you wear white? 'Yeah, although if u get white wrong it looks dead chavvy.' I double-tap like the message, and then worry I'm gonna get cancelled if he ever reveals I liked a sentence with the word chav in it. Then I feel stupid because, much like his view of marriage, Jack's use of the word chav is something specific to the reality of his locality. And when I feel disappointed that we desperately sought the right to marry, I often remember that it's not enough to be symbolically opposed to something – we have to think of the people's lived realities. The legalisation of equal marriage is something that smoothed daily life for a lot of people by giving them access to normality and by giving them access to rights.

Is my somewhat intellectual anti-marriage stance just middle-class smoke and mirrors? Is it perhaps of equal cultural value in my circle to be marriage-critical, as it is for Jack to be marriage-centric? Anything to fit in, right?

We talk about rights a lot, but what rights, if any, does marriage give you? We know the rights it affords heterosexuals: tax reliefs, inheritances, pensions, rights to kids and properties, travel and visas. While these feel like insignificant things for many thirty-year-old queers who are still living off the cash-in-hand jobs so many of us are forced to take, there are endless insidious ways our exclusion from the institution of marriage justified intense homophobic treatment in every aspect of our life.

Before equal marriage was legalised, it was fairly commonplace for gay people to be disallowed into hospital rooms to see their dying life partners, whether by hospital staff or 'family' (in the often useless, biological sense), on the grounds that the visiting partner had no legal rights. And they didn't. Cases like this were brought into relief hugely during the AIDS crisis, which changed the tack of much LGBT activism from being fairly unbothered about marriage, to realising the necessity for it within the system in which we exist. 'The AIDS epidemic brought gay men face to face with the consequences of legally unrecognised relationships. The illness or death of a "long-time companion" became even more painful when hospitals, funeral homes or government agencies refused to give any regard to the relationship,' writes Kenneth Jost in his essay 'Gay Marriage Showdowns'. In 2009 Janice Langbehn was refused the right to see her dying partner in a Florida hospital. 'The guilt of not being there to hold her hand at the moment of her passing has now been compounded by the fact that a judge says no laws in Florida can honour our family,' she told the *New York Times*. There are accounts like this all over the internet – people literally torn from their partners' bedsides explaining that they'll never recover from the sorrow of leaving them in their last moments.

Immigration is another silk in the web of how we've been structurally mistreated when it comes to our access to the legal side of love. In an article in *Out* magazine in the year 2000, it was estimated that 30,000 couples, according to the Lesbian and Gay Immigration Rights Task Force,

were split up because the US immigration system failed to
see that gay and lesbian partnerships were valid enough
to make a case for a visa. This comes, sadly, as no surprise
for a country whose immigration law banned homosexual
immigrants from entering the country in 1967 – a law not
lifted until 1990. It wasn't until 2009 that Obama lifted a
1987 ban on HIV-positive immigrants entering the USA.
Of course, there was a waiver – if you were married.
But since gay people couldn't marry, there was no waiver
for them.

Until 2005 gay couples weren't allowed to adopt,
because you had to be married in order to get a kid. This
complicates matters for heterosexuals who aren't married,
too, however being an unmarried heterosexual is a choice;
being unable to marry is not. Single-parent adoption has
been allowed since 1958 in the USA, yet were a couple
to split, the non-adoptive parent would have zero legal
claim over the child: a protection only afforded by divorce.
And in order to get divorced, you gotta be allowed to get
married in the first place.

There are examples of LGBTQIA+ parents as far
back as World War Two, but these are mostly in legal
documentation detailing how newly out homosexuals
and trans people leaving cis-heterosexual marriages were
denied access to their children. There are some more
heartening cases where visitation was granted, however
the visiting gay or trans parent had to prove they weren't
engaging in 'homosexual activity' (whatever that means?
Interior decorating?), nor could they be living with a partner.
In 1997 New Jersey allowed gay couples to adopt, but it
wasn't until 2010 that the last state – Florida, no surprises
there – allowed the same. Many US states continued to
disallow unmarried couples to have kids, and so countless

queer parents were disbarred not only from the institution of marriage but also from parenthood, until marriage was legalised in the US in 2015.

There's also case after case of absent families claiming entire wills, leaving lifelong partners completely broke. The same goes for the state taxing inheritances at a far higher rate for unmarried couples, in comparison to their married peers – both in the UK and the USA.

So while assimilation and co-option are important in deciding whether it's right to get gay-married or not, it's also worth remembering (I'm speaking to myself here) that people's gay realities don't always tessellate with anti-assimilationist ideology. I talk all the time about how we are not a monolith as a community, but I often forget this when I silently roll my eyes at gays who got married and post online pics of themselves atop the caption 'Gym with this one'. Okay, I'm sorry, but I just rolled my eyes while typing that, I can't help it. Maybe it's the gym, not marriage.

When you look at the scope of the injustice which stems from something that seems as accessible and as inconsequential as marriage, it would be a misnomer to name equal marriage as useless. Usefulness and radical are not synonyms, however.

So after all this: all the exclusion, all the fight, all the people who've never had their love tested before but got to have it celebrated since forever, I often wonder if queers are in fact more entitled to marriage than our heterosexual counterparts and we should look at revoking that right for heterosexuals. That would perhaps be radical.

For a start, not only were we punished for so long, we also actively saved the institution of marriage: both before our inclusion into it, and after. It could be argued that our existence outside of marriage gave heterosexuals their sole purpose.

'Family values.' We've heard that everywhere, this invisible thing that has been repeatedly used as a tool to deny us rights. 'What about the children?' countless conservative voices ask. 'Marriage is between a man and a woman.' Couldn't it be argued that the core values of conservatives only exist because we do? Perhaps in order to give the institution of marriage any semblance of meaning, the institution needed an enemy?

After the AIDS crisis raged in the west in the 1990s, the push to legalise equal marriage snowballed when corporate-aligned organisations like the Human Rights Campaign became the go-to 'gay' voice, and after much fighting in the Supreme Court and at parliamentary levels, (most) conservatives realised that their family values were more important than whether or not queers could get married. So instead of keeping us out and facing increasing dissent, we were welcomed into the institution under the guise that we would follow its rules. Many of those fighting at the front for this equal legislation to be recognised did indeed present an idealised image of the homosexual. We were just the same as those already allowed into the institution, with one singular difference in terms of desire.

But what about gender non-conformity, sexual non-conformity, what about working-class queers, or queers who weren't white, queers that were too weird to near approach any kind of normality? The problem with the passage of equal marriage is that inclusion requires assimilation into a system not designed to hold all of us. So while this was a momentous win, it was only one step in the direction of the liberation that so many activists of the

1970s and '80s were demanding. And really, in order to be included in the mainstream, the norm, the 'institution', it could be argued that you had to strip yourself of your non-conformity in order to be accepted. So winning the battle for equal marriage didn't, and doesn't, necessarily make us all equal. Arguably, the gay liberation movement lost its purpose: to fight for our most marginalised members, and alongside other allied causes such as the civil rights movement.

The fight for marriage left many behind because it didn't also demand healthcare, gender recognition and support for those impoverished, and it wasn't cognisant of the effects of our exclusion. Instead it simply sought our inclusion. And so we were co-opted by conservatives: just look at the increasing corporate involvement in Pride; the growing contingent of gay conservatives (we've all seen Twinks for Trump on Twitter); the rise of the transphobic LGB Alliance in the UK. Moreover, our equality on the world stage arguably created more inequality inside our communities. Our demands shifted and following our achievement of the right to marry, many who had fought for it forgot there was much other work still to be done.

That's not to say anyone is wholly to blame for this movement towards a capitalistic liberalism, but it is to say that the fight neither starts, nor ends, with Love Winning.

What's perhaps equally distressing is not just that queers were co-opted into a normative institution by a false sense of equality in the shape of a wedding dress and a diamond ring: we were also charged with the duty of saving it.

By the time we achieved the right to marry, the institution of marriage was in crisis. In the USA in 1960, 65 per cent of 18–32-year-olds were married; in 1997 that number dropped to 36 per cent; and by 2013 – just before gay marriage was legalised – that number hit an all-time low of 26 per cent.

There are lots of reasons for this fall, perhaps most notably the rise of third- and fourth-wave feminism, the global influence of the internet, and the staggering divorce rates among the boomer parents of us now marriage-age millennials. And so, as the clock struck gay and the White House and 10 Downing Street were lit up in the colours of the rainbow flag, countless think pieces, op-eds and research papers were published exalting the queers as the ones who might save marriage.

They all read the same: gays are better at communicating, gays are better at sex, gays are better at communicating about sex. One research paper even stated that as more gay couples start to socialise with straight couples (hellish! Can you imagine?), their enlightened communication habits might rub off on those emotionally stunted hets. The thing for which we had been denigrated over all these centuries, the tools many of us had developed in order to survive in our world borne out of exclusion, became the very thing people thought might save marriage. Love Was Love, and our love was, all of a sudden, exemplary.

A good example of how we might make marriage sustainable is with our much more fluid relationship with monogamy. In a 2015 survey by San Francisco State University, of 556 gay married male couples surveyed in the Bay Area, 50 per cent of them were in open relationships. In a 2017 study between the UK and Australia, of 34,000 couples surveyed, gay and lesbian couples were on average 'happier' than their heterosexual counterparts based on simple things like a more equitable approach to the division of labour and a more open discussion – with use of more humour, don't forget humour – around sex, jealousy and desire.

Mine and Ace's perfect Paris love became imperfect again when we were back in London, and in a gay pub in Limehouse watching a drag queen take bets on how many Jägerbombs she could sink over the course of the song 'Freed From Desire' by Gala. I knew the name of the song again, and the artist's, but Ace and I were pissed, so he didn't notice this time. And then he went to the toilet and was gone for a while, and in my head I imagined he was being cruised at the urinal – which he was, for about five seconds – and momentarily I was deeply hurt. Not by the act itself, which I find hot, but by the fact that some unknown boundary had been breached by him. By the fact that, for even a minute, I became, to him, the second-most desirable person in those rooms.

He dragged me into a cubicle and I thought we might have sex in there but instead he told me what had happened and we spent forty minutes discussing it in a pissy, cruisy pub bathroom while people knocked vigorously on the door probably seeking a space to have the sex we definitely weren't having.

Often when these things happen in our relationship – whether I've done something that breaches a boundary, or he has – it becomes a moment where we get to ask each other the questions we wouldn't usually have the energy or the inclination to. Instead of breaking up, these moments become a site for a breakthrough, in which we discuss our commitment to each other, as well as our evolving relationship with sex, jealousy and desire. And so the boundaries shift. Is this the kind of communication gay marriage could model? Were we the beautiful face of the New Institution?

Perhaps. Because indeed, there was a spike in marriage: in 2016, in the UK, there were 7,019 gay marriages. And as of June 2017 there had been 547,000 gay marriages in the USA. You can see both figures on infographics: a little uptick in what had been a continuous plummeting line, for the first time since the 1960s. There's not much data beyond that, although marriage rates in 2019 in the UK were back to being the lowest on record.

We did our bit to save this sorry institution, but in truth it was always going to take more than the gays and our forward-thinking attitudes to sex and communication to save the totally bastardised institution that is heterosexual marriage.

Sitting with my friend Lei one lunchtime, I asked whether he thought queer people deserved more of a right to marriage than heterosexuals. Usually fairly unbothered by matters of gay relationships, since he's not out to his parents and doesn't foresee a moment when that will ever be possible, he explained just how intensely infuriating he had found Kim Kardashian's 72-day marriage.

'I was shocked at myself to be honest, but I was seething with rage for three days thinking: if marriage is so precious that we're not allowed it, why are the most famous people in the world allowed to treat it with such cavalier disregard?' I laughed at this Miranda Priestly-ism but he was genuinely enraged.

We hear all the time this idea from our conservative detractors that queer people are too promiscuous, too obsessed with sex, to really understand or deserve an institution as sacred and ancient as marriage. The Pope waxes lyrical about the family, Trump called himself a traditionalist and has compared gay marriage to using the wrong club in golf, and countless Tories have said marriage is fundamentally between a man and a woman (I would name names, but there's like 136 of them) – and if we are to let gay people marry, we open the gateway to allowing all kinds of unsavoury marriages. We were told we weren't allowed nice things, because we'd ruin them. We were told our inclusion into the system would ruin the very system itself.

But this ruin has been, was being, done by heterosexuals long before our right to marry was achieved. Celebrity culture practically demands disaster weddings; you can get a $75 wedding at over 100 locations in Las Vegas alone, and 42 per cent of marriages in the UK end in divorce. This prized status was hardly handled like the cut crystal it's so often described as, and yet we weren't, and still aren't by many, deemed worthy of inclusion into that steaming pile of actual meaningless shite.

This cultural misconception – both that marriage has always been between a man and a woman, and that partnership is something queers can't understand because we're big sluts is completely off the money. Although it should come as no surprise that our part in marriage's history has been completely erased.

While many think this generation of LGBTQIA+ married people are the first of their kind to be married, queer people throughout history have been bending the institution since its inception. Both legally and illegally.

First of all, marriage hasn't always been an exclusively legal creation. According to the old-school version of marriage – in, like, the twelfth century – the Christian Church agreed on the principle that the only thing required to achieve wedlock was that two people vowed it to each other. They didn't need a witness, a ceremony or even a priest. It was the pair that actually made the marriage. And if overdramatic queers weren't declaring themselves married left, right and centre then nobody was.

When it comes to class and race, in the seventeenth century labouring-class people in the UK were often forcibly prevented from entering into marriage. Meanwhile, before the civil war in the USA enslaved people weren't allowed to marry. But in both cases many of those prevented would still live as husband and wife. They knew their love to be akin to marriage, and that recognition from an institution was meaningless, when the thing that makes a marriage – even today – is the love.

Nazi Germany, apartheid South Africa, the Church of England and, obviously, the British Royal family have all invalidated and disallowed marriages based on the 'wrong people' partaking in them. George IV, the Prince of Wales, married Maria Fitzherbert in private, but was forced to marry again because Fitzherbert was a Catholic. And of course, that was a matter of succession too: he couldn't have a Catholic wife because he couldn't have a Catholic baby, because that Catholic baby would grow up to be a Catholic king or queen. Hence the creation of morganatic marriages: where any resulting children can't inherit titles/assets/property if the kids, and the wife (their mother), are of 'lower status'. These are often very much a class issue: if a man and woman marry across classes, the posher party can ensure that their assets are safe.

But people did it: people who got married away from the eyes of others with just one witness, and you can bet your bottom dollar that queer people married in this way.

As with anything fun, self-marriage was made illegal – under the Marriage Act of 1753. Naturally, dissenters did it anyway. As so many of us know, the law doesn't always dictate our behaviour – and if it did I would have avoided countless comedowns, lots of sex in public, and the extreme guilt I felt for a year after I stole a Miss Sporty lip gloss from Boots, Lancaster.

So of course, if you look back in history, there are loads of marriages that happened that were never allowed. More specifically, there were loads of gay marriages – especially between women.

It depends also on what we mean by marriage. There's an endless history of Indigenous American, African and Asian cultures which includes same-sex and trans marriage. There are highly ritualised recorded practices for same-sex love and their unions in the Mesopotamian Almanac of Incantations, which was written, like, 4,000 years ago. There are stories throughout ancient Greece, and a few in Egypt. In the Ming dynasty in the southern Chinese province of Guangdong there are countless records of women binding themselves to other women, and men doing the same. There was pederasty in ancient Greece (where an older man and a young boy have a short partnership, a practice often, but not always, held in equal regard to marriage). Ceremonies of adelphopoiesis, literally meaning 'brother-making' took place within, and were approved by, Catholicism in Europe until around the fourteenth century, when Christianity began to conflate marriage with procreation for seemingly no good reason. And sadly no matter how hard we try, bum sex rarely makes a baby.

Chaucer describes this sworn brotherhood between men – where men would literally wed men in devotion to each other. It's hard to find out what a lot of these unions actually meant, and a lot of historians are quick to point out that there may not have been bumming involved, but if you want to tell me that Emperor Hadrian and Antinous weren't doing anal then you've got another thing coming. After Antinous died, Hadrian was so distraught that he spent years in mourning: building statues, naming flowers (gay) and stars (gay!) and athletic games (gay!!) after his deceased (air quotes) 'best friend'. I'm sorry but the only way to secure that kind of devotion is with the good dick. (What's even more camp about Antinous is that because Hadrian had built so many statues in his name he was eventually deified and worshipped as a god by a cult that spread throughout the Roman Empire until the end of the fourth century – and there's nothing gayer than a cult! The original stans!)

What's wild about history is that we take heterosexual sex as a given, but homosexual sex is often invisible unless overtly stated. The history books often read something like: We cannot possibly infer from their intensely worded letters, and a lifetime of cohabitation, and countless chapels painted in his/her best friend's name that he/she was gay. Trust me hun, if there's even a gentle inclination in the air – let alone a chapel/book/shared house – they're gay-fucking.

There's examples in Portugal, in Italy, in France, of men who married men and lived as 'husband and wife'. This was, however, much less common among men than it was women – because misogynistic homosexuality laws (irony is not lost) decreed that women couldn't possibly have sex with other women, so it was often easier (and legal) for women to shack up together and bang behind closed doors. This was a practice which became punishable by death for men in 1533, then by a lifetime in prison in 1861, then finally made legal, although deeply socially stigmatised, in 1969. But because women weren't afforded such visibility, throughout history there are glorious examples of women who married women – although often via acts of trickery where one of the party would dress up as a man, and present like that thereon. There's probably some gender stuff to unpack there too, but it feels anachronistic to say these people were non-binary or trans.

Some fave examples include the middle-aged widow Trijntje Barents, in Amsterdam in 1641, who fell in love with the younger Hendrickje Lamberts, who dressed as a man. Apparently this improved their sex life, according to Faramerz Dabhoiwala's book *The Origins of Sex: A History of the First Sexual Revolution*, in which it's written that 'Barents later confessed – the younger woman "sometimes had carnal knowledge of her two or three times a night, just as her late husband had – yes, and sometimes more arduous than he".' Blue really is the warmest colour. 'In the 1680s, Cornelia Gerritse van Breugel disguised herself as a man in order to wed her long-time lover, Elisabeth Boleyn, in an Amsterdam church. They were only found out years later, when Cornelia tired of wearing men's clothes.'

Examples like this rage on through history, with accounts in England, Germany, Holland and the States – some with letters back and forth between family stating their approval and love, others where troves of home-made dildos were found after the death of both partners. We absolutely love to see it.

These marriages weren't really so rare, either. Speedy marriages were easy to come by in London, for example, until Lord Hardwicke's 1753 Marriage Act, which condemned clandestine marriages. Before that, however, people could get married semi-secretly in brothels, taverns, prisons. According to Dabhoiwala, on 15 December 1734, a couple in Soho named John

Mountford and Mary Cooper decided to tie the knot. The first priest they approached refused to do it because he 'Suspected 2 women'. But they would easily have been able to find another priest. A few years later, a London minister performed the wedding of Elizabeth Huthall and John Smith; 'a little, short, fair, thin man, not above 5 foot', is how he described the person he thought of as the groom. Afterwards, he wrote 'my clerk judged they were both women, but they left as a legally married couple.' Again, we adore some lesbian trickery.

So we gave marriage back its cool, even momentarily. And, naturally, we're the most fascinating thing about its history. But it's worth asking the reverse question: what did equal marriage really give us? Sure, we got rights and a feeling of inclusion, but it's so often the case that a change in legislation doesn't always positively alter people's lives as it's supposed to. Did gay marriage cure all the ills it created within our community?

'I'd always wanted to get married, but by the time it was passed I had lost all faith in anything of the sort,' my friend Matthew tells me over a coffee. 'And beyond that I had lost countless partners who could have been what they call "marriage material" because we were never able to conceive of a future for ourselves. The fight that marriage gives you, the responsibility to your relationship that marriage gives you, was unattainable and on numerous occasions, when things got tough, relationships fell apart with nothing bigger than us keeping it together.'

It wasn't all raining corks, and chavvy/classy white suits (depending how you wear them). For multiple generations of queers, by the time equal marriage was passed, the cuts were too deep and the institution had not only lost its appeal, it also looked different to how many had expected it to be.

There are lots of articles on the internet about people who got gay-married and then gay-divorced. That's equality, and it's also a tragedy – with a fair few op-eds about how applying the model of marriage to their queer relationships, some up to twenty years' long, made the relationship fall apart.

But the most interesting are those who got gay-married after fighting for it, and found the whole thing quite remarkably anti-climactic. Like my friend Dillon. An avid activist, community organiser and father to three little gaybies. 'We got married on a whim – a kind of mad rager where the ceremony wasn't the centre of the whole thing. And it was lovely, and it didn't feel like as radical an act of love or protest as we'd expected it to be. It was a year after we were allowed to, and it was fun. At best. I actually got a bit too pissed and then had the worst hangover guilt the next day. Same as ever. But then when we left the place we'd had the wedding, my now-husband and I were walking down a street in London holding hands and a group of teens started chanting "Kill the Batty Boys" at us over and over. I'm not really afraid of threats like that to be honest, but it was a stark reminder that all the energy I'd put into gaining these rights hadn't really done much for us on the fucking street. That felt weird.'

But sadly it's not weird, it's precedented: when a huge legal shift occurs what often happens is the visibility of the group in question increases. Yes, there is no social group in the west in the last decade that has made more legal progress than the LGBTQIA+ community, but that – combined with a huge spike in online visibility whether via social media or artsy publications who love to pay us to write about our trauma – means there have been more covers, articles, viral posts and highly attended pride parades by us, and about us, but not always for us.

Because while heightened visibility certainly has its virtues when it comes to the education that exposure brings, as well as allowing many queers to access money and work in ways previously inaccessible to us, it arguably creates more violence too. Now people know what we look like, and as our voices got louder, so did the voices of our enemies – and the desire to shut us up.

It might come as a surprise that recorded homophobic and transphobic hate crimes, including stalking, harassment and assault, have more than doubled in England and Wales since 2014 – the same year the equal marriage bill was passed. Often when I've discussed these statistics before people have been quick to point out that perhaps we as a community are more emboldened to report these crimes today. But frankly, our community's distrust in the police has only grown stronger over recent years, and of all of the queer friends I know who have been assaulted, verbally and physically (and that is every single one of my queer friends, and I have a lot of queer friends) I can think of only one who reported the crime. When I was hospitalised on my doorstep in 2015 my friends and I decided it would be far too much hassle, and there would be far too much machismo to deal with, in going to the police. We felt safer going under the radar.

This surge in homophobic and transphobic hate can't all be traced back to our new right to marry, but there's nothing that says increasing power like being allowed into the most hallowed heterosexual institution. And with increasing power comes increasing visibility and increasing resistance: from governments, from conservatives, from people on the street who never once thought of a queer person until they saw them on a Netflix show, or on the cover of a magazine or newspaper.

Visibility is important, but it's not the same as social change. Nor did the ills that affected our community before marriage – the aforementioned alcoholism, depression, homelessness, drug abuse – abate after we gained these long-fought-for rights. The statistics are there, and they are rising. I'm not going to write them here, because they are deeply upsetting, but for anyone who doesn't know what the hard parts of being LGBTQIA+ in the UK are today, start by reading the LGBT in Britain Health report, accessible via the UK charity Stonewall.

So we were kept out of marriage and then charged with saving it by the same structures that had charged us as illegal and mentally ill less than five decades before; we made marriage cool again; we were erased from its history and debated over in parliament; we were deemed unworthy by so many and still are. And so it's hard to work out what marriage really did for us. It would be unfair to say it caused the increase in the problems in our communities, but it certainly created divides – and our visibility became as problematic as it was positive.

The picture is somewhat bleak. While my straight friends from home question why on earth I wouldn't want to get married, I try to remind them gently that while the biggest stresses of their search for love might be finding the right person, ours is very much the same, compounded by the fact that we as a community, and as individuals, suffer far more to find our happy-ever-after. And if you're lucky enough to consider marriage with a partner (if that's what you want), there's also the great fear that by engaging in this new-found right you are forgetting what the real fight is: it's for those members of our community who need the rights, and the privileges, we don't have. So while my friends search for the perfect dress, we search for the moral sacrifices we'll have to make in order to gain legal rights and celebrate queer love.

When I think about my potential wedding day, I feel a smack of guilt that by being subsumed into normality, by privileging myself, I will be actively dis-privileging others, abandoning my community and taking rights that other people can't get because they find intimacy and commitment hard, because their immediate concerns aren't relationships, because they can't be out to their families or because they are desperately seeking healthcare. Or because, for many of my friends, getting married as who they are would be impossible.

Yes, naturally, even under equal marriage, not all marriage is equal. This is the case for Hatty and her girlfriend Margo. Margo is a trans woman and is keen on getting married. But because self-identification is such a giant hurdle, one where you have to sit in front of a board of cis people and give evidence of who you are in order to clear, many trans people don't bother changing the gender marker on their legal documents. This means that in order to get married legally, Margo would have to do so as her sex assigned at birth.

Sure, this might not be felt on the day – with far more marriage contracts now involving gender-neutral pronouns like 'Spouse A and Spouse B' lol – but technically under the 2004 Gender Recognition Act Margo's marriage to Hatty could be annulled if Margo were ever to seek a legal change in her birth certificate. The same would be true for myself: there's no actual possible way to define legally as non-binary, so while I'm sure it wouldn't affect proceedings so much, who knows what kind of dysphoric emotions the process of trying to slide myself into a system designed originally for a man and a woman, both assigned as such at birth, would bring up?

And so equal marriage doesn't feel so equal after all, because equality is a chimera when trying to work within a deeply binary, normative system. We find ourselves back in the 1970s, with the same wants and needs of activists then, wondering if marriage is really worth it or whether abolishment is the only option.

Yes, it's nice. Queer joy. Queer love. Queer celebration. They're all deeply important to a community who isn't often allowed that. However, not only did the law-making heterosexual gatekeepers fail to reckon with the effects of exclusion and erasure on our communities across centuries, they also failed to consider that giving us symbolic equality in one arena does not cure the countless inequalities in others. And so our joy remains limited. As Dillon said, even the luckiest of us, who get to have fun on our wedding days, can't be protected from the danger that waits for us out on the street, beyond the reception venue.

Normativity polices what is normal. It creates classes of citizens, to get Marxist about it, and the underclass lose out drastically both socially and structurally. Marriage is one of our most effective metrics for the ways in which classes of citizens are defined and then confined to those definitions: working-class people couldn't get married, then they changed that; enslaved people couldn't get married, then they changed that; interracial couples couldn't get married, then they changed that. And marriage will change again: being that change is the only constant in its mis-told history.

Right now, gays find themselves at the frontier of this changing legislation, but in order to engage with marriage responsibly we must look at the underclass our inclusion into this institution creates: who is left out and what effect will that have on them? Only once marriage expands to include all conceptions of relationships between consenting people maybe Love Will Really Win, and Love Will Truly Be Love. And maybe then, those phrases won't sting so much.

But for now, I'm off to a gay wedding.

3

The Queer Opiate?

SOFIE AND OONAGH ARE the kind of people you're genuinely happy are getting married. Both, like me, grew up in isolated towns; both, like me, grew up with confidence-debilitating awkwardness; both, like me, grew up queer and feeling undesirable. As potential loners, much like myself, you can't help but be glad they've each found their weird, loner lobster.

They're very knowing and responsible about their white female queerness, both obsessed with intersectionality and cognisance of their own privilege (although we can still quote *Sex and the City* at each other as if gospel).

Oonagh works at a big women's media company, but is constantly on the brink of getting fired until another feature piece about butch-dyke aesthetics she fought tooth and nail for attracts more traffic to the company's online platform than anything else that month. Sofie is a video game designer. As you might assume about a video game designer, she's pretty odd, but radical and smart and compelling in the way that introverts tend to be. With Sofie it always seems like she has the most well-observed and incisive thing to say: someone who uses a select few words correctly to say what I might chat shite about for seventeen minutes. Instead of using her few words at their eventual wedding, she would read a passage from an Ali Smith book that she thought perfectly summed up her love for Oonagh and then they'd both cry like teenagers, and so would I.

Sofie and Oonagh are also the kind of people you can't quite believe are getting married. They used to be allies in the drunken dinner party fight for non-normative modes of romance and coupling. There we'd sit, multicoloured hair, offensive quantities of make-up, over some outrageously tough beef that one of our friends had tried to cook so that we might feel momentarily rich in those post-uni overdraft years, creating the illusion of eating in a restaurant because staying in was as boring as being heterosexual. We'd prop up each other's twenty-something-year-old *Guardian*-reading opinions with the smugness of a rebel army who truly believed they were set to take over the world. The food was always dreadful, so we'd replace it with the much less complicated booze and sit screaming about politics into the early hours of the morning, lighting cigarettes from cheap scented candles, losing our eyelashes in the process.

Before 2014 we'd rail against the homophobes. 'How can it be the Lord's Year 2014 and queers still can't get fucking married?' we'd all howl at each other like harpies, trying desperately to find some rhyme or reason, and some humour too, in our barring from the system. Back then we all wanted marriage, inclusion, 'the same rights as everyone else!'

Then the Tories passed the equal marriage bill in the UK that same year, and then same-sex marriage was legalised across the US by the Supreme Court the year after, and for a hot sec everything was rainbow. Now that it was ours, we went from savaging the equal marriage naysayers to tearing down the institution.

'The queer opiate,' I would call it. 'Fucking scumbag politicians making us think we have it all, but we're still getting beat on, we're still dying, we're still illegal in over seventy countries,' the dinner party attendees would concur. 'Did you know that donations to LGBT charities in the US have more than halved since the passage of equal marriage?' my friend Amelia would tell me. 'People think we're done!' A year later I'd find myself beaten to a pulp outside my home in east London, feeling smugly vindicated and deeply heartbroken at the same time. As if proof this brutal were needed that we are certainly not done.

Pre-2014 we'd dutifully retweet articles about marriage equality, we'd go on marches, Oonagh and I would write thinkpieces and interview queers about why these laws needed to be passed. Now we were publishing interviews and articles about people who thought marriage would be the death of queerness. As the confetti-littered wind changed, so did I: I would be pro-marriage until its legalisation, and firmly anti-marriage thereafter, desperately clutching for any system against which to fight. And now, as time has gone on and loads of cool queer folks are saying 'I do' in small, trendy town halls and celebrating in relaxed cocktail bars or gentrified working men's clubs, I find myself firmly on the fence.

But when it comes to marriage you can't really be either/or. Half in and half out – it's kind of a done deal the moment you slip the ring on the fing. So when it comes to marriage you're either political ... or married. Surely not? Oonagh is fervently invested in politics – identity, geo, party – and I can't imagine all her years of reading, talking and fighting dissolving simply because she's dissolved into the structure of marriage. Perhaps Oonagh has more to fight for now than pre-vows? Perhaps the promise of forever means you can visualise it and if you've publicly chosen it you're more likely to go to battle for it? I struggle to think of an equivalent commitment, other than marriage, that signals a forever.

Two months later, smoking outside a cafe in south London with Ace, debating this very point, I was proved right. Despite his vehement anti-marriage conviction, neither of us could think of another way to really show your commitment to another person forever. A kid? A house? Oddly, nothing feels as concrete as marriage does in securing the couple itself. 'Donating a kidney,' Ace suggests – something we both agree we'd do for each other in a heartbeat. 'But that's a matter of life and death,' I say, 'not necessarily choice or commitment.' And so we're back at marriage.

The master's tools will never dismantle the master's house, as Audre Lorde wrote so deftly. And marriage is the ultimate tool in the master's armoury, because it's the ultimate tool of mastery. Well, we had chosen to be our own masters.

The day of Oonagh's marriage to Sofie had arrived. Admittedly, this was my first gay wedding, and as I tried to apply my mastery analogy to the beaming pair – something that is easy to do at a heterosexual wedding – I couldn't quite work out who was mastering whom. With straight weddings, at least as far as cliché goes, the initial feeling is that the man masters the woman. Or is the cliché that the woman masters the man, with cooked meals and an arm rub when a fight needs winning? Of course this is not all marriages, and there are some formulations of heterosexual matrimony that completely flip the script (more on that later). But what's always apparent about these structures, whether in favour of the man's or the woman's control, is that they're decidedly gendered – the woman often using her labour, or her 'feminine skills' or 'wiles' to control the man.

A lot of my heterosexual female friends are constantly contending with the idea that they are marrying into the patriarchy, so much so that I have a few gal pals who have become proper political lesbians. To them, being trapped in an eternally gendered battle was too close to their idea of hell, so they abdicated their heterosexuality.

Perhaps I'm being too simplistic. In any case, trying to apply the same gender structure to Sofie and Oonagh – the one I'd learned from the married couples I was surrounded by growing up – didn't work. It's also quite comical that I found myself falling into the trap that we so often make fun of straight people for: trying to 'crack' who in a same-sex relationship is the 'man', and who is the 'woman'.

Here, there was no evident master, just two rad queer women in love telling people that they were. Imagine a sort of reclamation of gender roles, very camp and very knowing: wherein Oonagh leaned toward the wife end of the spectrum and Sofie became groom-like in her aesthetic.

Oonagh had on a beautiful dress and less-conventional boots, Sofie wore a very masc-chic suit. From the feeble throwing of the bouquet to the speeches, gender was both mocked and ironically embraced, and everyone was in on the joke. Already this seemed more appealing.

The pair are aware of the lesbian stereotype of one butch one femme, and so they love to cheekily assume space within those categories – Oonagh is a femme, with a butch sensibility, and Sofie is what they call a soft butch – masculine, yet reserved (think Kristen Stewart but Danish). So from the outside, to the 'normal' viewer, today was a day much like Sam and Abi's wedding, where gender is omnipresent, but this time its subversion was the toast.

Among the guests there were still certain impasses on the whole gay thing: there was a Catholic uncle whose face was thunderous all day, although Oonagh and Sofie know what he's like and derive a sick kind of strength from it – the same strength queers learn to draw from bullies whose minds are much smaller than ours, safe in the knowledge that karma is a bitch, that that kind of behaviour won't take them a tenth of the distance we could go. And even though we were at a gay wedding, people couldn't cope with my pronoun either, because both families are liberals: finally happy with a gay daughter, but not quite sure how they feel about trans and non-binary people. I didn't make a fuss; this was still a nice, normal day, after all. And I couldn't be bothered with watching people's faces mangle as they tried to compute what a fucking they pronoun is. So I necked the Moët, because I love the Moët. Perhaps my pronoun is Moët?

The pair can't wait to be wives. 'There's no template for us,' Oonagh had said a week earlier, as we sat outside a niche cupcake shop in Mayfair before beginning our hunt for her wedding earrings. I see her point: there's no template to what a long, happy gay marriage looks like, and so it's an exciting, perhaps queerable unknown. And that's what Oonagh knew. Perhaps this was where my judgement of the couple came from – from jealousy, from insecurity that I still didn't know. From the fact that somehow Oonagh and Sofie had managed to divorce their personal from their political, and be happy in the fact that they were getting married because it made them both feel happy. End of. Neither of them seemed less political – their intentions to change the world still set, but now with rings on their third fingers. In fact, coming from a Catholic family – helmed by two parents who grew up working class, in a small village in a small county in Northern Ireland – could it be said that Oonagh's choice to have a gay wedding was political, in context? Identity politics comes in many forms – whether in campaigning, engaging with online activism, or by introducing subtle changes to those around you who otherwise would never have seen or attended a gay wedding. Exposure to difference is a critical part of gaining acceptance, which is why I tell my mum about getting gangbanged on a dance floor in Berghain, and why Oonagh wanted her devout Catholic family at her wedding. It's a shame that even a day lauded as the happiest of your life becomes political, but Oonagh can handle it. She, like me, thrives on it.

In terms of the marriage itself: yes, the form might be normative, but couldn't the content be queer? Never mind that Oonagh and I had spent months scouring wedding sites, jokingly sending each other clippings from copies of *Closer Brides* – which actually had some pretty good ideas – because we knew we were taking the piss. Apply that thinking to other things, and it holds up nicely: clubs themselves aren't queer in form, but fill them with queer people and the space becomes a queer one. Sex isn't queer in form, but put a dick in the bumhole of a man and all of a sudden it's queer.

So what about marriage? Not sure. Perhaps I'm not sure because nothing about queerness for me has ever been finite or concluded – its very point is the asking of questions – and perhaps the finality of getting married feels, by nature, too conclusive ever to be queer. It's also a kind of riddle of contagion: will marriage catch queerness if queer people marry into it? Or will queer people catch convention if they marry? Who's rubbing off on whom? Who holds the power to change the other?

Maybe the queering of marriage isn't about what you do with the institution itself once you're in it, but more about its importance in your emotional biography. Eat Pray Politics Marriage. In that order. In the west we're taught that marriage is one of most important things you'll do in your life. It's a milestone, an emotional goal that decrees success in the eyes of others because you're a Good Enough Human to warrant someone wanting to spend the rest of their life with you. But perhaps a way to queer that very process is to reorder where marriage sits on your priority list, as just another thing you do. Or to marry a wanker and get divorced in a day, Britney-style (very queer).

Of course, this isn't just a queer conundrum. Plenty of my heterosexual friends are also questioning the institution, trying to work out how to make it relevant, or irrelevant, to their material, spiritual and political lives. Some of them – like my friend Emily – are more fervently anti-marriage than most of the queers I know. Perhaps because she's a child of divorce, or perhaps it's for feminist reasons, or perhaps because she wants to fuck around a tonne. She's also just never really felt the urge to consider marriage, let alone do it. When we first met at uni, I was of course doubtful of this decision and would question her to the point of fury, believing that she didn't really know what she was on about. 'Everyone gets married, Emily!' I'd say, because – in my life up to that point – everybody had.

Then there's my friend Eve, who got married last year. She's a really good ally, someone who is avidly feminist and wonderfully supportive of her queer mates. She even joined the London chapter of ACT UP because she wanted to donate her energies to HIV activism, which absolutely lies on queer, female and racial lines. But she wanted to get married. It made her and her partner happy, and everything about their wedding, from planning to action to clearing up, was about the collective celebration and not about Being a Bride.

I interrogated Oonagh about how she was planning to make her wedding and her marriage queer and she shrugged, while holding a pearl drop earring to her left lobe, and said something about how her skin looked like shit, 'and just before the wedding, too'. Oonagh – sidebar – has written expertly on beauty standards and skin positivity, as she's a sufferer of adult-onset cystic acne, and she's smarter than this, I think, so it feels odd that she's descended into skin insecurities like any old bride. And so structure creeps in.

I try again, ten minutes later – 'How are you going to do it differently?' – and now she's concentrating on the question because she's finally found the perfect pair of earrings. She says, 'I don't care. It's us. That's different enough.' This makes me think: even in the most normative marriages people choose to elevate their love as special, as different – for all the cookie-cutter weddings there are, in each case it is that couple's supposedly 'special day'. Maybe 'it's us' is actually enough if you believe it. From the outside my partner and I look like two white men nearing thirty. Sure, I think our internal life is rich and different from other people's, but is it really? We love watching *Friends* together, we adore cancelling plans, I hate it when he hangs the washing up lazily and it smells like dog when it's dry. Maybe what a wedding day represents is what we all truly crave – to feel a little special in a life that's basically not. Maybe marriage, now – not historically – is actually all about ego. About feeling special and believing you really are. Every wedding I've ever been to is based on this assumption and even the most thoughtful of wedding greetings cards still say things like 'On your special day' or 'To the special couple'. Perhaps it's simply redoubled ego that prevents me from wanting to get married – I'm hanging on to the idea that I am different. But isn't that just the other side of the same coin?

Impossibly, both pro- and anti-marriage perspectives feel utterly essential to me, biological: as though I was both born to get married and have evolved to detest it at the level of my DNA. Not that biology is destiny of course – otherwise I'd be a large male lumberjack – and this opposition to marriage feels deeper than a political vanity.

Oonagh then tells me about the moment she knew without a doubt she wanted to marry Sofie. Autumn light streamed in through a window in their home, as they ate vegan Danish pastries. Oonagh says, 'this was the first time in my life I felt like it all fit ... so cheesy,' but it makes me cry.

I think about sitting atop Arthur's Seat at Sam and Abi's wedding with Ace, and how I felt like it all fit then,

too. 'But is fitting enough? Is fulfilment enough?' I quiz
Oonagh. 'It is for me,' she says. And in that instant, in
what's been such a loveless world for people like Oonagh
and me, I believe her. And I'm thrilled for her.

I don't begrudge Oonagh this, the way I might if I were
talking to a hard-heterosexual. Of course, people who
identify in all sorts of ways, even the most conventional,
have problems, as well as a right to get married, but I know
Oonagh's particular pain in many ways – of wondering
whether it's possible ever to be fulfilled because you've
spent so much of your life imbibing the message that
you're an unloveable freak. To find an antidote to all that
is something worth cherishing, loving, holding on to, and
perhaps even marrying for. I celebrate Oonagh and people
like her getting married, because I believe she deserves that
happiness more than most, because she's felt the opposite
way for a very long time. I believe this is Oonagh's version
of belonging, and I trust in her intention to rewrite the
rule book. Do queer people have, on account of our being
disallowed and unloved by society for so long, more of a
right both to celebrate and be celebrated for their love?
Yes, obviously, is my initial answer. However, choosing
who has more right to anything is what got gays into such
a mess in the first place. And so, no, in real terms, nobody
has more or less of a right to marry than anyone else.

I stop asking Oonagh questions and we laugh about old
times and how stupid we were, and as we say goodbye
we pretend that next time we see each other something
monumental won't be happening. Yet the atmosphere is
weighted with a sense of significance; that we're waving
off our youth, drawing a line beneath our naivety, bidding
farewell to the constant nagging worry about where our
next STI will come from.

Fast forward a week, and I arrive in Twickenham alone, in shorts and a pale lilac woman's jacket because it's a gay wedding and now I can wear whatever I want. And for the first time in five years, I haven't spent the morning getting ready for a wedding in a near panic attack because I have to squeeze my multitudes into the male corset, better known as the suit. The difference feels palpable, and the content, thus far, is feeling more catered to someone like me. It's the same day as a big rugby game, my fave, so I spend a good twenty minutes navigating hordes of drunk men, worried about my visibility, thinking – perhaps for the first time ever – 'I can't wait to get to this wedding,' while I can hear my heart beating in my ears.

Guests arrive through Oonagh's parents' house, which is folded deep into the tree-lined streets of Twickenham. We're shown out into the garden where there are flowers and wicker chairs and a white gazebo that looks like it's sweating in the early September sun, much like me under this jacket.

They walk down the aisle and I cry like a plump mum, which is, frankly, what I am. They kiss and raise glasses and for a moment it feels like gender could be anything, and like I am witnessing a moment in history, both personal and social – despite there being plenty of married gays out there – because it still feels, frankly, non-normative that two women could marry and kiss and hold hands and be toasted the way my friend Sam had been just a few months before. It had broken my heart to realise some twelve years earlier that this reality wasn't something I could count on. And so, to see it now was a kind of indescribable nourishment, something that felt hard-won, weighted with a history of fighting.

As they walked through the crowd to make a speech, I started to cry ... again. I cried for my friends, I cried for everyone like us, before us, who wished they could have done what Oonagh and Sofie just did with someone they loved, and I cried for the little people within us who spent years pining for acceptance and normality. I cried for a thirteen-year-old me who thought I would never be happy, who was terrified and weak and would spend the next decade being ever further weakened by external pressures and voices. I cried for the idea that mums and dads could love a gay child – something that should be entirely usual but is entirely not. I cried because Oonagh and Sofie looked fulfilled in ways that drugs and fags and shags and leaving the party at six in the morning never quite seemed to do for them.

Oonagh spoke about this very fact, about this particular moment as something she once thought impossible something which had changed in our relatively short lifetimes. She read a passage from a Michelle Tea book, then looked those of us who are queer directly in the eyes and talked about our right to marriage, our right to happiness, but how we must absolutely remember who put us here. The Gay Liberation Front, ACT UP, Peter Tatchell, Marsha P. Johnson and Sylvia Rivera, Stormé DeLarverie, Harvey Milk, Audre Lorde, queers, femmes, queer femmes of colour who are lost to an irresponsible history. Those icons who fought for us to be able to live as we are.

As the day rode on, and traditions were upheld and subverted in an assortment of ways, I found a smoking buddy, a woman whose name I never got even close to remembering. She reminded me of my Auntie Rita because she had the same hacking I'll-never-quit-smoking cough, a northern drawl and hair so lacquered it was a rock-hard shell. I idolised Rita: both my auntie and the one right in front of me with the square hips, the flesh-coloured tights and the court shoes that created a wobbling line of divots in the lawn.

Northern women have an inspiring ability to sunbathe literally anywhere. When you grow up in colder climes, it's a given that the moment the sun peeps through the clouds you get your bra straps down and crackle, even if for a matter of seconds. Rita (not my auntie, but Rita 2.0) spent the day darting around to find the sun rays, cavalierly smoking around and on everyone whether they liked it or not – very me – and so I spent the day following her lead because I was infatuated. Over the course of the wedding we talked in depth about lots of things: Laura Ashley, contraception, shagging, the tube and how she hates it, why she likes to iron her bed sheets, voodoo (which I told her wasn't hers to practise, she didn't listen) and, of course, weddings and marriage.

Rita was pleased with this wedding. She devoured the Greek chicken and the fish pie as if she'd not seen a hot meal in weeks, and when I left out the prawns in my serving she reached a wrinkled, sun-spotted hand across the table, fag still in it, and scooped them up, smudging mashed potato all around her chops as she chewed loudly, and talked even louder. I'd never really seen anyone smoke with their mouth full, but Rita did and my god it was inspiring.

As a general rule, Rita had seen enough of weddings. She had been married twice, once widowed and once divorced, and she was pretty happy with how things had turned out for her. She wouldn't get married again, she revealed, but reassured me that the marriages she did have had their perks – 'one for the love and one for the money.' She told me that marriage can be a transactional process, one of convenience, one that doesn't have to be for overwhelming love but for any purpose you see fit. She had successfully rewritten the importance of marriage in her emotional biography, which felt radical for a seventy-year-old northern working-class Catholic woman. In a financial bind in the 1990s, for example, she married for money and while she repeatedly refers to her ex-husband as 'that fucker/bastard/wanker', she says it was one of the best decisions she'd ever made. She could live because he'd been able to provide.

More inspiration from Rita: that marriage can be something mutable – something that doesn't have to be sacred or done for the 'right' reasons. Ace and I are both financially barren, so if we married it couldn't be transactional in that way. But perhaps it could be frank and honest in the way we'd approach it. Something full of opportunity for exploration and subversion and sex with other people, rather than an unquestioning commitment to one person and one way of life, without an acknowledgement of our practical motivations, too. Perhaps we can make marriage belong to us, rather than try to fit inside it. The question then is, what would be the point of doing it in the first place?

If I'm completely frank, were I to be in an open relationship I would need a bind like marriage – something that feels bigger than us – to be able to trust completely that Ace and I remained at the core of it. But I can't imagine pairing something so conventional with something so unconventional, unless it's the colours red and green in a particularly well-schemed outfit. And perhaps the solution to a constant worry that someone might leave you oughtn't be marriage; we've just been conditioned to think it is. Perhaps the solution instead is therapy, or time, or conversation, or perhaps it's a constant and immoveable part of the human condition that we cannot know the future, whether married or not, and we should just accept not knowing. Perhaps this is what makes relationships, still, so enticing: the interminable mini-torture of it all. Is this why marriage can, ironically, kill relationships? The security burns away the play of tension?

I left the wedding early after my friend Katy had gone on a rampage to pick up coke from a dealer she was also shagging. Iconic. I love Katy so much, but coke isn't really my scene, so I slunk off into the night after saying a speedy goodbye to Oonagh and Sofie (who are also the queens of the French exit, and so understood). On the everlasting train home from Twickenham, I thought about the pressure of finding the right spouse and how so often the want to marry can eclipse finding someone who is actually right for you. We've all been to that wedding where you know, wholeheartedly, that your friend is marrying the wrong person. We understand when people are trying on for size things that are patently bad for them in short-term relationships, but it's a whole other thing when they're seemingly so blinded by the desire to marry that they take the inappropriate person down the aisle. This exposes something about their deepest desires, which are strong enough to cloud their judgment. I wonder what this exact desire is – why it is we are getting married when we don't really know why?

And funnier than this phenomenon is how dissing a bad husband or a wife, or a non-binary spouse (the English language fails, once again), comes at much greater cost than dissing a bad boyfriend or girlfriend or partner. Even if it's to those who don't believe in marriage so much, and even if it's coming from those who don't either: because we've all been taught to respect and revere marriage – even if we don't know it.

As far as I'm aware, all my friends love Ace, so I don't need to fear that my desire to be wed is blinding me to his patent unsuitability, nor that in watching me propose to him, my friends would all be struck dumb by the terrifying institution of marriage to tell me that I'm making a grave error.

Because Ace is wonderful, friendly, smart, charming, very attractive and hilarious. He gets hysterical with laughter at least once a day, and he weeps and weeps and goes tomato red when he does, which in turn makes me do the same. We share the same politics; we have practically identical left-wing values, as we formed most of them together, and so it feels like we're a good match, like we mirror each other well. That said, he's terrible with money – worse than me, only somehow we've developed a dynamic where he borrows from my teeny-tiny reserve. He leaves the Weetabix out every single day and I have to put it back. Every single day. It angers me to think that not once has he made the connection between where he gets the Weetabix from and where he leaves it. Two years ago, when I was holed up in my childhood bedroom in Lancaster writing my first book because I couldn't afford an Instagrammable writers' retreat, he called me very early one morning to reveal, in a rightful panic, that he'd got with two strangers in a club bathroom while really drunk. Our relationship with monogamy had always been more monogamish – both of us having participated in group sex together plenty of times. And while ideologically the act itself was okay, it was more that we'd never discussed the reality of sex with others when there's only one of us present.

It felt like the Weetabix thing again – an incredible act of thoughtlessness. Nonetheless we never even talked of breaking up. We're older and wiser than our high-school selves who said 'dump him and move on'; we understand that one transgression or broken rule isn't sufficient to bulldoze the amount of work you've put into erecting, in every sense, a loving, joyful, supportive relationship. Instead, we did work – work on him, work on me (because these things don't happen in a vacuum) – and we moved forward. We still talk about it regularly and if anything, it's deepened our understanding of each other and has proved the strength of our bond. I also find the visual of him getting with two strangers in a loo incredibly hot, kind of like how you want to fuck your bully at high school.

This, then, is a marriage to me. The goal of so many people I've known is the wedding. Sure, that is exciting and big and strange – but to so many of my heterosexual friends, especially those from up north, I've never really heard them talk about marriage. It's all weddings. For me, I'm more intrigued by what comes after – by what changes and what stays the same. To me it's important that the emotional place where a marriage begins is not as deep as the place it moves to. A relationship is not simply stasis, but moving together – and if I'm committing to eternity with someone I need an absolute promise of that movement. Ace's cheating on me was more of a promise than other things in our relationship, oddly enough. Sofie and Oonagh had changed almost unrecognisably since I first met them, and they had grown into each other's change together. And perhaps committing to that movement, that change, is a queer take on marriage.

When I got home, after nearly missing the last train towards south-east London from my connecting station because I was so busy standing still while thinking about moving, I accidentally (on purpose) knocked Ace awake when I climbed into bed with him, champagne-drunk from the wedding, and asked him if he was really anti-marriage. 'Yes.'

A short answer. Damn it. 'How can you know, though?' He muttered something about wanting to go back to sleep, and then I said that he was deflecting, and so he sat up and turned the lamp on and held my hand and said, 'If I was going to marry anyone in the world it would be you. Does that help?'

No. I wanted to know why his views on marriage were so unshakeable. His parents hadn't married until their late sixties, and did so resentfully, for pension reasons, and were known for rallying against the stupid system – but even they'd done it, eventually, and when pushed, admitted to enjoying it. They're part of a cool art-school 1970s crew who all checked out of normality with their first tab of acid. Norman, Ace's dad, is a rabid socialist and has decreed anything that upholds the system we're in – like marriage – to be unquestionably, absolutely disgusting and pointless. Ace's mum Sarah was more interested in sleeping with married men than becoming a wife. She was wholly committed to second-wave feminism, smoking fags and taking pictures of rock stars. When they met, Norman, who's from a tiny town in the most northerly part of Scotland, had been married very young, as was, and still is, the way in many small, working-class communities. He'd

run away to London, become a builder and a socialist and
had a kid with Sarah. They both had everything they'd
wanted – fun, parties, art, cigarettes, booze and a baby –
and they both enjoyed rebelling against their parents who
desperately wanted to see them tie the knot. Ace grew up
like this, in a house that not only didn't assume marriage,
but actively discouraged it. I asked if he thought that
getting married would actually, in a sense, be doing what
they did, rebelling against what his parents wanted for him.
'Why all of this now?' he asked, to which I said nothing.

I can't sleep and Ace won't talk to me. So I go to the loo
and google 'scientific reasons to get married' and all that
come up are pieces on sites like CreditDonkey.com that
say things like 'matrimony protects your heart'. Naturally
I'm repulsed and so I put Google down and head back to
bed and think about Rita.

Rita's insights were helpful, but I felt like they only half-
applied to me. I lie awake for about three hours reflecting
on different permutations of marriage, and I can't think
of a single person near to me whom I could ask about
open marriages or poly marriages, or even not-normal
marriages. I sneak into the bathroom with my phone
again and sit for an hour googling open marriages and
poly marriages, upon which I discover polygamous
marriages are legal in more than double – sixty-three –
the countries that gay marriage – twenty-three – is legal
in, and I think that's cool, and then think that I'm perhaps
fetishising cultural practices I know nothing about. And
then I think that it's fucked that gay marriage is only legal
in twenty-three countries and then I feel a whirlpool of
contradictions start to engulf me.

Then I remember this director I interviewed in LA
about four years ago who was in a proudly open marriage,

whose rules were postcode-based: you couldn't fuck anyone in the same postcode, but after that all bets were off. He was a kink-porn director and so it kind of figured that the rule was pretty loose. I dig out his address from the depths of my inbox and send a deranged email telling him I'd like to 'quiz him on his queer marriage', which at 4 a.m. I think sounds kooky and fun. I realised in the morning that kookiness is perhaps one of the traits I most hate in other people, so I sent another email explaining properly why I wanted to speak to him and he got back to me straight away telling me that he and his partner had got divorced. 'The postcode thing didn't work out,' he joked – but he'd be happy to link me up with a bunch of his married, open friends, 'some fags, some hets,' he added. I agreed.

4

Married to Freedom

'I WANNA FUCK DUTTY and he wants to fuck vanilla,' Amir explains over Skype. I laugh – such a strong opener – but Amir doesn't find it funny. 'Okay ... not a joke then?' I enquire. 'No. We fuck different, but we love each other, and so we knew from the off that we'd be open. We haven't actually banged in ages, but last year we spent three-hundred-and-sixty-one nights in the same bed. And I got topped by about ninety guys. It works.'

I was connected to Amir by my porn-director acquaintance. He is delicate, no facial hair, with incredibly toned but thin arms. He kind of purrs as he speaks, like a sexual cat that wants to be fucked but not an actual animal because that's weird. But yes, Amir wants to fuck – he wears a tight vest and is in his pants, which he shows me: they read NASTYPIG on the waistband. His neck is padlocked by a thick chain, denoting a dynamic of ownership: kind of like a wedding ring, I guess. I don't ask whose padlock it is but I assume, perhaps wrongly, it's his husband's.

It's here where I get stuck. Now, I grew up in what might be described as your 'normal' family – Mum, Dad, siblings, money stress, meals eaten on our knees while fighting over what TV we watched. And marriage, like in most 'normal' families, was the glue of the whole unit: Mum and Dad were married and monogamous (although of course for a lot of 'normal' families monogamy is a well-maintained illusion), and in the times when it was very hard it seemed like it was those vows that kept them together. More than, perhaps, any love or want – a social pressure was placed on us all to fit the mould. It wasn't until I left home that I really realised that other conceptions of families, of relationships, of ways of being, existed. I became aware that the idea of a 'normal' family was something archaic, stifling even, to the real potential of what human relationships could look like. Of course my family was, is, wonderful. But the nuclear family is a deeply heteronormative, patriarchal, colonial ideal: the white, suburban, heterosexual family.

Amir, a slutty, sexy, sub gay man is the polar opposite of this in so many ways: he seeks potential, a life lived in the pursuit of pleasure. So it baffles me, then, that he chose even to engage with the idea of marriage. Of something so normative, so socially acceptable. Even their gay marriage is – while hard-won and different – still marriage. But if Amir is going to reject social convention with such keenness, why get married at all?

I'm not baffled by the open bit, of course. I have friends who are in open relationships, and I've dipped my own toe in. I can completely understand the mentality behind polyamory, and sexual openness – much like liquorice – is not for everyone, and neither is monogamy.

But meeting Amir, it's clear to me how wedded (sorry I'm a pun-loser) I am to the concept of marriage as synonymous with 'normality'. Already, only ten minutes into our conversation, I can feel that familiar discomfiture when you realise you've been wrong about something. Perhaps because I was raised in a family with marriage at the centre, I'd always just assumed that it would all be fun and games and dicks and fannies and hot loads all over my face in dark rooms or the loos at Westfield Shepherd's Bush until I finally settled down and got married, when all that would stop.

I assumed that when I was married I would find everything I needed – sexually, emotionally, financially, culinarily – with one other person. Of course I'm now aware that finding everything in another person is a fallacy and that so much of what you need comes from your relationship both with yourself and with others to whom you might not be romantically linked.

Even so, with everything I've witnessed in this elsewhere world, I still think that if I were to get married I don't know quite how I'd negotiate all the emotions that come with both an open relationship and a convention like marriage, which I've spent so much of my life venerating. To me it had always seemed to be a choice: stay weird or get married. Not both.

'I've never been one for marriage,' Amir crackles on my computer screen. 'Not for political reasons, I just always assumed people who liked to get fucked like me, who liked

85

the idea of getting fucked by loads and loads of men all the time, would never find someone who wants to develop an intimate, no!, committed relationship with them. And then I found Stan and he wanted that and I understood that urge, and so we got married and didn't think too much about it. And our openness is the site of least contention in our marriage, perhaps surprisingly.'

'Least contention?' I ask, surprised and, frankly, doubtful. I must seem like a nun to Amir, my eyes visibly widening when I have a question about his set-up. Despite having my share of sex with others while in a relationship, for some deep-set psychological reason I can't fathom how that can work in a marriage. God I'm so traditional.

With Ace we have an agreement: we technically aren't allowed to have sex with other people, although – as evidenced by both of our actions on various occasions – it's case by case. We are allowed to have group sex when we travel to other countries – in dark rooms in Berlin or Madrid, for example, moving seamlessly through the barrier of monogamy into something more exciting.

But perhaps these all feel like the fumblings of people who found each other young and aren't quite ready to commit fully to each other, monogamously, forever. The prospect of that sounds terrifying, and the idea of our sexual expression being something that belongs only in our youth is both ageist and idiotic. So, now I'm at a juncture in my life where I have all these marriage feelings for Ace, but I also feel terminally unsure I can commit my body, my sex, to one person forever. Could it be possible to do both?

'The first thing to consider is trust. You have to trust that, after you've been barebacked by a tonne of guys in a hotel room off a highway on the outskirts of LA, you can go home and trust the thing at the centre of all this is still intact. It's like a contract,' Amir explains, when I ask him what the first rule of being in an open marriage is.

Thinking back to our fluid-filled flights of fancy, Ace and I do already have this kind of contract: no anal, no kissing. I take this ring. Once – in Budapest – we were really drunk after a night of red wine and lángos (don't recommend), and I kissed this man, passionately, while Ace was at third base with him. Our fugue state was swiftly punctured, and he stood up and stormed out, me following sharply behind. I forget the details of the subsequent conversation, but it was something about how important these rules – the no anal, no kissing ones – are, if this monogamish set-up was to work. 'Whatever the rules, if pre-agreed they must be closely followed,' Amir advises.

He's right. Even if they're as catch-all as 'don't tell me anything' or as specific as 'don't get with anyone on a weekday after 9 p.m.' – because the complicated, fragile nexus of trust must be woven strong as a tapestry if the central relationship is to survive divergence from what we grow up understanding conventional relationships to be. And the thing about tapestries is that if you pull on a thread, the whole thing can unravel.

'We fight about how we prioritise work over each other or what movie we want to watch or who our favourite drag queen is or money or dumb stuff like that,' Amir rolls his eyes, 'but the sex thing is something we understand about each other, and something we feel pretty smug about. You know ... that we really did that. We have some rules, and we follow them strictly, and it just works.'

I love conversations like this: ones where people have such a wildly different conception of the world to you. It would be nice to get there, I think. But in honesty, the reason Ace and I haven't quite reached openness like Amir and Stan have isn't for lack of desire, it's because we're really nervous we might ruin what we have. Worried we might, while fumbling around in the grey area, break our contract and fuck it up. It almost makes monogamous marriage look easier: a simple, one-step rule of don't fuck anyone else.

We all have the friend who went open and their perfect relationship fell apart. Mine's my friend Emery, who had nurtured an idyllic three-year monogamous relationship with her girlfriend. They were the kind of couple we all thought would make it: they made dinners together, and painted walls in various shades of Farrow & Ball together. They were forever people – the kind who go to Peckham Salvage Yard and invest in a piece of really good furniture – and they would happily tell their array of literati friends over long, middle-class dinners featuring much wine, much conversation and much cocaine, that theirs was a relationship for the books.

'I think for us, going open was a mixture of things and maybe we each did it for different reasons,' Emery explains over the phone. She's since moved to New York – a very glamorous, very Emery move. 'I think we both questioned whether we believe in the idea that monogamy is really the natural or right way of doing things, or whether it's a social construct: and wanted to put that to the test. Especially as queer people in the habit of questioning received wisdom or inherited traditions. I think for me I felt like I met this person too young and wasn't ready to stop exploring the world in a sexual way – or having new romantic relationships. I wanted those things, and thought "why can't I have them while I'm with my partner?"'

Emery always makes a good point. Perhaps the most important one there is the one about received wisdom: because who says what wisdom society gets to hand out? It's a conundrum we'd often try to wrap our brains around at Emery's famous dinner parties: who says so? Who decided gender is binary? Who decided relationships are heterosexual? Who decided love was monogamous? But of course, as received wisdom and social conditioning often does, these questions answered themselves for Emery and her girlfriend.

'Jealousy, insecurity, lack of communication, naivety, carelessness,' are the reasons she gives for their falling apart. 'You have to be really secure in your relationship and yourself in order for it to work, to trust the person, and to trust your own feelings. We are very different people and dealt with it in different ways – I took to it quite well, but it – and maybe my behaviour – made my partner feel insecure.'

Part of me wonders if one of the reasons I have such a keenness to get hitched is to shore up some of that security Emery says was lacking in her relationship, before it fell apart. Because once that legally and socially binding contract is signed, agreed upon in front of blubbering mums and tutting friends, my tense relationship with trust, with jealousy and insecurity – of the kind felt by Emery's partner – might relax somewhat. In truth, trust isn't something I necessarily doubt within mine and Ace's relationship. We've been together five years, and the trust we've built has grown roots. Perhaps, then, getting married might be an effective catalyst to help us explore the desires we have for other people, sexually, or, who knows, emotionally? If Emery's relationship fell apart because of unresolved insecurities, then perhaps marriage is the kind of societal seal I need in order to solve my trust worries.

But really, what are these trust worries? Ace has cheated on me in the physical sense, I've certainly cheated on him in the emotional sense: sharing a little too much of myself here and there with friends or crushes, knowing at the time that where the conversation is going feels like something that should be reserved for just Ace and me. Don't we all cheat in some way? Don't we all lust after others, secretly stalk someone on Instagram and think 'if the opportunity presented itself maybe I wouldn't say no'. Don't we all omit certain interactions, or flirt with someone when you know you'll never be caught, or feel really good when a stranger slides into our DMs saying they 'saw you in Victoria Park in your bomber jacket' and that they 'find nothing sexier'? We all cheat, maybe it's better to recode this cheating as far more normal than handing over your entire sexual and emotional self to someone the moment you agree on monogamy. And it's fun!

'Honestly I didn't feel that weird about the sex either,' Emery explained when I brought up the matter of Ace's cheating, stating that I didn't really feel that bad when he did it. In fact, I felt quite the opposite: turned on, perhaps even jealous – but in a good way. This feeling is known as 'compersion' – where we find joy or pleasure in knowing that our partner is happy, expressive, receiving pleasure with another. Why would you not want that in a marriage?

'It was only when my partner said they were developing deep feelings for the other person that I felt pangs of jealousy and insecurity: that felt like a much bigger threat to our relationship,' Emery added, after telling me about this girl she'd just fucked with a strap-on in the Bowery. (That's glamour.)

The thing that rings true across all these relationships that went closed, then open, then ended, is that communication, or lack thereof, is so often the thing that falters. It's not the doing of the thing, or the doing of the third person, it's communicating about it in a way that doesn't reassure your partner that they're still the priority. Sure, the very act of Ace sleeping with someone else made me feel like I'd been de-prioritised, but the fact that – when the drugs and the booze and the post-coital euphoria wore off – he chose instantly to focus on working on our relationship? That made me feel secure. And the rules – that Amir and Stan dedicatedly uphold, the same ones that faltered in Emery's relationship – are a kind of priority, right? That even when you're sleeping with someone else the rules that you created with the person you're prioritising stay concrete. Because really what is a relationship if not prioritising one person over many, both in your mind, your bed and your calendar? Maybe that's received wisdom too, but 'commitment' – which is what a relationship is, which is what marriage is – is basically another word for 'priority'. (Although if you google synonyms, other words for commitment are actually way bleaker: obligation, duty, tie, charge, liability, burden, pressure. I'll take priority.)

It's here where western society's demand for monogamy cannot hide in plain sight: because monogamy is a system that demands we prioritise one other so the state doesn't have to prioritise us. Monogamy, and by and large, marriage, is a niftily constructed system which allows those in charge to neatly organise those that the state should care for. Marriage eases the state's responsibility to you: it means that when you get old you'll have someone to care for you, or when you have a baby there'll be people to care for it. Thus we can work for each other, protect each other, nurse each other when we get old, all in our neat family units – and then we die and the state haven't had to do all that much to take care of its people. That's why non-monogamy is so frowned upon in a social sense.

And in terms of desire, marriage and its cementation of monogamy is another means of social control. God knows what the world would look like if desire were prioritised, if pleasure were prioritised over the achingly dull, morally valuable idea of being 'good'. We've all heard of the ruckus caused by swingers clubs in suburban villages, the twitching net curtains and exchanged bodily fluids, and most of us have been party to that painful method of psychological control that is slut-shaming. But to imagine the chaos that would ensue if society were structured around pleasure rather than purity would force us to imagine a new world order. One that I find, frankly, enticing.

Of course, I'm not exactly saying this current world order is constructed by the government in power right now, nor am I saying there's an architect of this sat somewhere pairing us off like chess pieces and cackling loudly every time his marriage clock chimes and another couple somewhere are stripped of their desire and desirability. What I am saying is that such a lot of our social traditions, the teachings in our schools, the depictions of marriage, monogamy and divorce in our media and culture deem anything but that to be shameful, a failure, a moral misgiving. And so we get married (monogamously) to fall in line, to avoid the prying eyes and the word 'spinster' being branded onto us like the bare naked NASTYPIGS we are.

I was shocked that I didn't feel more catatonically hurt by Ace's sexual misconduct. He, however, was wracked with guilt that he'd hurt me. That he'd hurt the relationship. But it wasn't really me he had hurt; it was more a relic of me before him, one which had always paraded around a hard line that if someone were to cheat on me they'd be out on their ear! 'Once a cheater, always a cheater!' I would say to my friends from high school all the way through university. But then, after university, I met more people like Amir, and fewer people like my teenage self (thank god), and realised that cheating, openness and monogamy are not as cut and dry as Rachel from *Friends* once told me.

To be fair to my naive former self, that relic of me was back around the time where relationships were lived between myself and a mirror (a pretend boyfriend), a time when my bible was *Sex and the City* and my straight female friends turned to me for (ill-informed) advice because while they were busy fucking the town fuck-boys, I was busy eating ice-cream solo and weaving myself into the world of Carrie Bradshaw, soaking up every line as if it were god's given truth. If I couldn't be in love, I would become its oracle.

This is what we call the Peter Pan effect – among my friends at least – the delayed romantic development of many queer people like me. All of us, whether from small towns or big cities, were starved of romantic opportunity throughout our adolescent years because people were either straight, or gay but pretending to be straight. The hostile landscape of high school, of gay teenagerdom – an experience presided over by fear, mainly – wasn't really conducive to the formation of young love in the way my heterosexual best friends experienced it. The first time my friend Lauren found herself in reciprocal love was when she was fourteen; the first time I found myself in the same state was at twenty-one. That's nearly a decade spent wondering what that experience was like, mapping ourselves onto the Drew Barrymores and the Molly Ringwalds. And, while so much of me had matured past the ages of adolescence, the first relationship I found myself in exploded because both of us were adults acting like teenagers. Me, learning on the job how to deal with all these wild feelings that really didn't fit with what I'd come to understand love to be. I'd believed the movies and the TV shows: the ones which decreed we must stay up all night talking, be comfortable in each other's silence, be breathless at our partner's touch, fuck seven times a week. When these things didn't materialise I took it to mean that something was wrong with me, rather than something being wrong with how love is portrayed across mass culture, how the world is telling you from year dot that you must fall in love, be all-consumed by it, and then never stray from it. Considering the world watches 165 million hours of Netflix a day (which is, holy shit, nearly 7 million days', or 18,835 years', worth of TV streamed worldwide in a day) I'd wager (on the conservative side) we spend 75 per cent of that time swallowing normative ideas of love and relationships.

Lei, a friend who's approaching thirty, has only been in one semi-serious relationship – something frowned at, idiotically, by society but something totally usual in the queer world. He puts it down to Peter Pan syndrome. 'This manifests itself in the very teenage act of putting boys on pedestals and really admiring them in a very teenage way, like the girls on *The Hills* do with their abusive boyfriends,' he tells me as we sit on his roof, while we guzzle the most teenage idea of an adult alcoholic drink – a cosmopolitan (maybe we haven't fully shaken off the Carrie Bradders hangover). 'I think it comes from the complete lack of actual experience or intimacy with men. And the only concept that you develop is entirely from mainstream fiction. Specifically, very "girly" depictions of how we must be with our men. And there are no depictions of gay men doing that, just teenage women whom I aspired to be like. To the letter. Obviously I had no practice since I learned that when I was a teenager, and so when I had my first relationship it fell apart because I let him walk all over me. Like Heidi on *The Hills*. But I'm an East Asian gay man. The same rules don't apply.'

Lei is right, and I learned, through three or four relationships of varying lengths and varying levels of drama, that cheating, or any sort of 'betrayal', wasn't necessarily a deal-breaker like it was in those TV shows we so relentlessly binged on. It was all about the context of the betrayal, of the obstacle. That's a kind of nuance you're not getting from popular culture. A man can be a pig (not in the good, Amir-type way) – unsupportive, gaslighting, borderline (if not outright) abusive – and that can be acceptable on TV and in the movies; but if he cheats, even though he is as good to you as Ace is to me, that means we have to break up?

See, this betrayal or obstacle might be completely at the fault of one party in the partnership, but Ace's transgression, for example, was something symptomatic of wider issues stemming from how we'd been communicating. Or, more accurately, how we hadn't. The cause, in this case, didn't necessarily justify the effect, but what effect is justified when one person in a relationship (me) isn't pulling their weight? Ace and I make each other happy, we love each other very much, and what this obstacle created for us was a pause on our partnership – one which made us stop and evaluate, first of all, whether we really wanted to be in this relationship. Once we answered that with a resounding yes, more questions arose about how we could heal, how we could work out the root cause of this thing that was making him feel bad, and me feel turned on. Of course there are scenarios where a transgression like this would mean it might be time to leave, to end the relationship. But that depends on the relationship's parameters: for Ace and me our monogamy parameters were loose, and in the past we'd played around the region of openness, just together. We'd even discussed the idea of being fully open in the future: aware that sexual desire for a solo partner might perhaps ebb and flow, and further aware that the idea of monogamy for the rest of your life – just because you decided on it when you got together at twenty-four – seemed like a ridiculous choice that someone in their twenties might not necessarily have been equipped to make.

And if all goes to plan with our newly set parameters, and I still want to marry him like I do now, why can't these two things coexist? The problem that's clearly afoot here isn't that I'm scared of openness or lifelong commitment, it's that I revere marriage as an institution. And while there's a part of me that wants to get married for the security, the trust, the contract, the very same part of monogamous marriage terrifies me. Sure, I can see myself gladly sharing my life, my bed, my money and even my skincare products with Ace for the rest of my life, but the idea of sex with one person, forever, until you die? That's one of the biggest turn-offs when it comes to monogamous marriage. Never would I be able to hear the half-satisfying/half-terrifying click of the door latch when entering a Grindr meet's marihuana-filled apartment again. Never would I have the strange thrill of having sex with a complete stranger, not even caring to learn his name – let alone remember it. Never would I have the sensation of a differently shaped penis inside me, or taste the subtle deviations in different people's cum.

I find it far easier to wrap my head around the idea of being non-monogamous and not married, than being non-monogamous and married. This makes even less sense because the things that worry me about going open – the failing to prioritise each other, the falling in love with someone else, the worry that your person who is sleeping with another person (while you sit at home and watch *Buffy* and reheat the second half of the Covent Garden soup you saved for them) may or may not still love you – are seemingly banished by my idea of what marriage is. Commitment. Contract. Trust.

I sat down for brunch with my friend Cris, a queer person who's in a double marriage that's also open. I wanted to work out both the practicalities but also the feelings that came with being in an open marriage. If Netflix isn't going to give me depictions of non-monogamy, I'd have to find them out for myself. And where better to start than in Dalston, over a Cobb salad and a cigarette.

'Basically we are a four, and we're in love. We all live together and fuck together and sleep together in different formulations each night – like one of us might sleep alone if we need space, or we all might sleep in one bed after date night,' – a tight squeeze, I think – 'and we got married.'

Cris is very queer: visually, emotionally, politically, so it surprised me that they had also decided to get married. 'Well, we aren't technically all married – we drew names out of a hat and the person's name who we drew was the one we married. It felt like a big Fuck You to the system, while also allowing us to engage in this thing we'd all fought for as queer people.'

I jokingly asked them if they had a preferred partner, 'like a name you were wishing for when you put your hand in the hat?' but they seemed offended by this, and for the rest of the brunch spoke to me as if I wasn't quite getting the point.

'We all got married on the same day, at the same time, next to each other, so while I married Ben and my other partners married each other, we held hands in a four and said "I do" at the same time and kissed each other and so it essentially felt like we all married each other. All our mums did readings! Except one. But she's dead.'

This feels wild, but also kind of pointless. Why not just not get married, if the very practice and structure of marriage (as we know it) is something you're out to defy? 'Well, I think it was most important to me, frankly, because I'm from a Northern Irish Catholic family and marriage was something I always wanted. And it was amazing – ironically, it still really pleased my mum that I was getting married even though it wasn't religious and it was to two guys and a non-binary person.'

'What is the limiting factor then? What limits does marriage allow you to put on the relationship?' I asked.

'There isn't one. Look – the limits of marriage didn't stop us from finding a way. Why should marriage be a limiting factor? Shouldn't it just be some kind of commitment and celebration? It's absurd that we handcuff ourselves to a single person forever. That's lunacy.'

Cris is right, really, although I know I won't be going up north to my mate Gemma's wedding and shrieking 'monogamy is wrong!' when asked if any of us object. When I think about marriage between Ace and me in this context, after meeting these people, it's something I guess I can imagine will be an opportunity for openness, rather than the signifier of closure. After the cheating chat had subsided and I'd had time to assess what I actually felt about the whole trust/betrayal thing, I'd found myself confused that my trust in Ace had grown stronger than it was before we'd stopped at this checkpoint in our relationship.

And what about jealousy? Or mistrust? I ask Cris. 'I just feel happy for them. And more attracted to them, knowing that others are attracted to them too. Honestly. It makes life way more exciting.'

Now, there aren't many statistics around open, swinging or poly marriages and there are perhaps even fewer examples of them depicted in culture. It's something you certainly have to seek out – most likely before you're married, or, if you've said the vows but are looking for openness, then perhaps sometime in the dark, after your spouse has gone to bed.

In one *New York Times* article, published in 2011, Susan Dominus wrote about a couple who had opened up their marriage. It was as binary as you'd imagine: man likes sex, woman less bothered, man wants open relationship, woman doesn't. So they give the open thing a go. Then the woman is diagnosed with Parkinson's and meets a man at a support group who is living through something similar.

They end up kissing, and the original couple end up near breaking point. Until the woman offers to give up her extra-marital relationship to save the primary partnership – to which the husband says no. Things swiftly shift, and the pair establish a connection that seems far superior to fidelity: one founded on honesty, respect, transparency. Both parties in the primary couple admitted that, after the near-break and subsequent opening of their marriage, they became happier in it, more awake within its parameters.

Some of the statistics that exist on non-monogamous marriages seem to reflect an increase in happiness after their opening. One 2000 study, by Bergstrand and Williams in the *Electronic Journal of Human Sexuality*, reports that of 1,092 people surveyed, all in some form of open marriage, 80–90 per cent found themselves 'happier' after they opened up their marriages. And 50 per cent of those who reported they were 'very happy' before their marriage went open, said they were 'even happier' thereafter. In Timothy Wolf's 1985 book *Two Lives to Lead: Bisexuality in Men and Women*, 76 per cent of open marriages surveyed were reported as being 'outstanding' or at least 'better than average'. The statistics are, obviously, quite hard to gauge though because how do you test the happiness of a marriage? For every one study that says marriages are way better, more functional, when open, there's another which says they are Satan's tool and will most certainly lead to divorce. There are also a few that take about nineteen hours to read and at the end are just like: 'inconclusive', 'neutral'. That's time I'll never get back.

Before the West colonised so much of the world, understandings of marriage and relationships were much more fluid than what we see before us. In fact, non-monogamy and polyamory have far more cultural precedent than monogamy. In Mesopotamia, ancient Egypt and ancient Greece both polyamory and, more often, polygyny was practised as the norm: one man, many wives. In non-Christian religions like Islam and Hinduism, this is still contemporary cultural practice in many parts of the world. In parts of Nepal, polyandry is practised – one wife, many husbands (iconic), and in parts of China there are walking marriages – where you can have sex with anyone you want. Monogamy is not hardwired into people in any sort of natural way, it is merely a product of the culture around you. Not to say that other forms of marriage don't have their issues and imbalances, but it's foolish of any of us to imagine that what we think we know is correct.

The first contemporary cultural touchpoint for open marriages in the west came in 1972, in the form of the bestselling American book *Open Marriage: A New Life Style for Couples* by Nena and George O'Neill. Then AIDS happened, Reagan happened, Thatcher happened, and everyone was a monogamous conservative terrified of pulverising such socially entrenched family values. Look what happens when you do. Of course, people eventually realised that GRIDS (Gay-Related Immune Deficiency Syndrome) was actually AIDS, and anyone could contract the virus, and they also realised Reagan and Thatcher were both walking nightmares (although it seems a lot of us have forgotten this in recent years).

So ideas of open marriage went away – although of course they still happened, they just weren't making it onto the bestseller lists. Until Janet Hardy and Dossie Easton released their 1997 book *The Ethical Slut: A Guide to Infinite Sexual Possibilities*: free love, with a caring heart, was its raison d'être. In 1998 we got *Sex and the City* – the show that raised me, the show that also probably made me an Ethical Slut. And proud. In 2004 we got *The L Word* – in which there were loads of open relationships. We had *Swingtown*, *Big Love*, *Sister Wives*, *Secret Lives of Women*, *The Girls Next Door*. In 2020 the BBC released a scripted series called *Trigonometry* – a show whose sole focus was about opening up a marriage.

In 2012 Dan Savage coined the term 'monogamish', and brought the idea of non-monogamy to his podcast and its 200,000 avid weekly listeners. And we can't forget the growth of the online realm, porn and dating. According to Pornhub's statistical insights for 2019, threesome and gangbang porn are among the twenty most searched for categories, with threesome in the top five for men, and gangbang in the top ten for women. There are also apps that facilitate open hook-ups: LovingMore, MNPoly, PolyMatchMaker, OkCupid, Feeld app.

Statistics aren't everything, though. In matters of the heart they're often useless. I can read the statistics – with the help of my Stats GCSE and an open mind of course – and understand that open relationships or poly marriages seem to work on paper. But in reality? There are no useful stats or cultural touchstones to help stop you feeling what you might be feeling: the worry, the jealousy, the disconnect. And what happens if you love your partner, but fall in love with a new one? With that couple in the *New York Times*, it's interesting that it took them nearly losing their marriage to open it up: a sort of last resort. But what if the primary partnership isn't in jeopardy? What if it's great? Should I not be satisfied? Or should I be able to have my cock, and eat someone else's too? And once you've worked out the whys, there's the daunting prospect of the hows.

I decided to email Cathy Keen, the person in charge of community and events at Feeld app. Released in 2014 under the name 3nder (not sure how you say that), Feeld is a location-based social 'discovery' app that allows you to connect with people interested in polyamory, kink, swinging and other alternative sexual preferences such as getting jiggy with more than one partner at once. She replied straight away, up for a chat.

Cathy is kind of the face of poly marriage in Britain – not necessarily a hard title to get seeing as it's still quite taboo – but last year she went on *Good Morning Britain* (Piers wasn't there that day, thank Christ) and talked, with her husband and then-girlfriend, about poly marriages. We started with this.

'People ask stupid questions all the time, so let's not do that.' We don't. Instead we get into the nitty-gritties of Feeld. 'It's an amazing community. There's loads of users, and you can connect to learn about new ideas – like heteroflexibility, for example, in which there's been a 92 per cent rise on the app – or polyamory or openness. It's a really safe place. Much safer than Tinder, for example.' (There are lots of functions on the app to promote safety.)

I ask her about poly marriage. 'I think if everything I know now I knew back then, when I married my husband, we wouldn't have done it – it was an assets thing to be honest, because we had a little boy together. But now legalities are different.'

I ask her if she got married to have some sort of normality in her life. 'Maybe, maybe. To reassure my mum. Yes. Especially since I was a sex worker, I maybe just wanted to make her happy with one life choice I'd made. Obviously when she found out about the poly stuff it was less easy, but she's worked it out.'

We laugh for a second about mums and them working things out, and I ask whether – as she's seemingly quite over marriage now – she thinks the vows have held her relationship together in times when it might have been easier to walk away. She replies with a firm 'no'.

'But—' she stops me as I'm about to ask another question, '—being poly has. See, my husband's an alcoholic and that has been hard. Having other people in our relationship has given me support with that, it's given me places to find support both for myself and for him. People often think polyamory is a threat to a relationship, but in my experience my central relationship has only ever been made better by its opening.'

So Cathy makes a case for the idea that opening up a marriage can lead to a better primary relationship. If each party is getting more support, especially in the harder times, then perhaps it takes some strain off the central relationship. Perhaps it aids honest communication, and allows us to reduce our frustrations by talking about them with our other partners, rather than sitting on resentments the way so many monogamous couples do, before blowing up over the 'way he slurps his FUCKING soup' or the fact she 'hasn't taken out the FUCKING bin' or how annoying it is when they, like I do, 'drop their FUCKING dirty socks on the floor of the lounge EVERY fUcKiNg night!'

It was in the wake of cheatgate that mine and Ace's first serious conversation about marriage arose. We were talking on the outside stairs in front of our flat after we'd just got back from Sainsbury's. One of those intensely domestic moments you imagine are only reserved for films: choosing an unusually bland place to have one of life's Very Big conversations.

'Maybe marriage would be fun, like resisting what my mum and dad taught me. Think they'd respect that,' he said.

I raised an eyebrow. 'I don't want you to say that if you're saying it out of guilt.'

'You know, I'm really, really not.'

And then we made a spaghetti bolognese and watched *Will & Grace*, and I looked at him out of the corner of my eye and realised that perhaps his trust in me had bloomed too. At our lowest we all expect those whom we love to leave us. We expect to be punished for our actions, and that's how we create such a culture of intense shame and therein behavioural control. So when, in fact, my response to his cheating had been a mature one, one which he wasn't expecting, perhaps I, too, had passed a certain trust checkpoint in his mind. Like an unintentional test of sorts: for better or worse.

After the whole cheating thing was over, or as over as a significant marker in your relationship can be, I spent a while wondering why I was so swiftly over something I'd built up in my head over my entire life as the ultimate betrayal, up until this point.

Trust, I'm learning, isn't a binary thing in relationships. It's not an all-or-nothing situation. Do I trust Ace to be honest with me about his feelings? Yes. Do I trust Ace to take the laundry out of the washing machine before it gets that stale, doggy smell? Absolutely not. Do I trust him to make me a coffee every morning? Almost always. Do I trust him to always prioritise me? No way.

Until then I think the area of the trust spectrum I'd struggled with when it came to relationships, commitment, cheating, was more to do with trusting the fact that I was loveable enough to be in a relationship with; committed to, not cheated on. Trusting that someone could actually love me. The me who picks their nose and wipes it under tables, the me who has a nine-step skin routine and can't fall asleep without forcing my partner to watch an episode of trash TV he doesn't even like, then falling asleep three minutes in. The me who has been ghosted fifty times, rejected a hundred and fucked a thousand.

This is the same me who craves marriage as a binding contract to prove to me that someone can love me the way Ace does. But there's no proof of that, even with the promise of marriage because, as we all know, marriages fall apart almost as frequently as non-marriages do. And even when they don't, trust and love and trust that you are loved aren't automatically and unquestioningly present everywhere a ring or a marriage certificate is.

'I think there's actually more trust in my marriage, than in so many typically monogamous ones.' I meet Ebony, another friend of a friend, who lives in London. 'I'm married and asexual, but also polyamorous.'

'How does that work?' My face is twirling into a confused splodge, although I'm trying not to appear to be a total idiot. I imagine that it takes an open mind to get here, and a long process of unpicking and restitching all the seams of the normal lives we were trained to seek out from childhood. That received wisdom Emery was talking about. I always thought that the idea of nature and nurture applied to childhood alone: that when I first came out as gay, all the naturing and the nurturing had been done and I was here and gay and that was me done. But it becomes clear that over the course of a life full of questions, nurture never really stops having an effect. That you can be nurtured in any direction. And something about these widening conceptions of marriage seem to be hitting my nurture trigger. I like the notion that marriage can just be an experience, yours to do with what you wish. A place where desires or potential or new experiences don't end. A place that you can rework and rework until you work out what best serves both of you, and your relationship. But I still keep wondering, then, what the point in actually getting married is. Nobody can quite give me the answer to that, unless it's about assets, and as a jobbing actor and working-class writer, all I have to give in the asset department is debt.

'Well, I'm married to my partner who is also asexual, because we're in love and we understand each other,' she's smiling, 'but then we're poly too – so we're allowed to form emotional connections with other people.'

I ask whether Ebony is allowed to sleep with other people, and she tells me that obviously she doesn't want to and I apologise and say I'm sorry for misunderstanding asexuality. She accepts. 'But all of our connections with others can be as romantic as we want. At one point I think I was in love with about six people, and my husband with another two, and it worked like a wonderfully understanding and well-oiled machine. We're a little community of asexuals who fall in and out of love with each other, and the trust and emotional understanding runs deep.'

I want to know why Ebony got married in the first place, but she pre-empts the question and puts it down to 'just knowing' that her husband was the person she wanted to marry. I ask, 'Have you ever wanted to marry any of your other partners?'

'Yes. I've been engaged to one, even though we knew we couldn't get married. But I think with my husband it was just a way to commit to each other, to prioritise each other.'

I find this concept hard to grasp. Not on behalf of Ebony – I couldn't be more pleased that she's found a place and space for her own desires to be fulfilled, to feel held and seen and cared for. Everyone deserves that. But the way Amir, Cris and Ebony all speak about their open marriages gives the impression that there are no problems at all and that the reason for marrying in all cases was 'just because'. Amir says he'll never find someone like Stan and that he 'just wanted to lock it down', and Cris explains that it fulfils a deep desire. But nobody I ask can give me a reason to marry someone that's better than wanting it in order to fulfil something socially, either within themselves or their families. And wanting to 'just' do something is a good reason, sure, but it seems to me that these people with exceptionally politicised sexualities and identities are smarter than that, especially when that thing they want to do is something archaic from which they would typically be excluded. Amazingly to me, none of them seem to be fussed about the politics of getting married. They're concerned with the politics of what's inside their marriage, and think it's political that they're doing what they're doing within the institution itself, radicalising from within.

What about monogamy then? After all these conversations, my mind is slowly changing towards imagining a marriage that can actually be open. I'm realising that the prospect of marriage actually excites much more if you can imagine that opening it can serve it better. Both through having space to talk to others you're seeing about the things that trouble your primary relationship, and also, let's be honest, getting to shag tonnes of people: that's just good sense!

I decided to call my best mate Holly, from Lancaster, whose wedding is in three months. Holly is monogamous, Catholic(ish) and she's happy with her aspirations to normality, and happy that mine are the opposite. There's no judgement in our relationship, and so I wanted to get inside her thinking as to why monogamy is right for her.

'It seems like there are more rules in an open relationship, than in my, like, simple set-up?' She begins. How so? I ask. 'Well I've only read about it really but like people in open relationships can have really strict rules about how they go about it, but with me and Dan it's just one rule.' Do you ever dream of breaking that rule? 'No.'

I doubt that highly. I rephrase. 'Do you ever have moments where you look at your life stretched in front of you and want to, like, fuck it up?' Holly takes a moment to think. 'Yes. Definitely.' I'm surprised by her candour: my usual encounter with people in traditional relationships is that they are very defensive of these boundaries, of even being asked questions related to these choices. Perhaps that's reductive, but I guess it's similar to how I would get angry if someone asked me when I chose to be gay, or chose to be non-binary. But, hilariously, I get asked both all the time – and it's often the same people, when the question is reversed ('when did you choose to be straight') who can't fathom an answer. Holly isn't like that though.

'How often do those thoughts come?' I poke.

'Not so often, and less and less as time goes on. But I've always been really honest about how our relationship has played out: we moved in together really quickly, for financial reasons, for example. And sometimes I do think about what it would be like to have a first date again, to have sex with someone again, to do that with different people. But just because I think about it, doesn't mean

I want it more than this. And you know, I'm sure people who have chosen more open, or less traditional, situations than me and Dan also imagine the other possibilities. That's human nature.'

I ask Holly if monogamy, marriage, the house, kids, car, dog, were something she actively chose or something she slid into unquestioningly. 'I like all those things. I like the tradition in a way – it's what I know, and it makes me feel nice to be getting married in the Catholic Church that my grandma was such an active part of. Maybe I did slip into normality without asking too many questions, but a question I've always asked myself is whether or not I'm happy. And I am: I love my dog, my fiancé, my wedding dress. It makes me, for the most part, happy.' I laugh at her for saying she loves her dog before her fiancé.

'Do you think there's another formulation of this life – one where you're, say, in an open relationship with Dan – that could make you even happier?'

'Not for me and Dan, I don't think. Maybe if we broke up and I approached a new relationship with someone else, knowing what I know, I would consider it. Maybe. But it doesn't thrill me per se. The idea of a wedding, a marriage, stability: that does.'

Why?

'I dunno. I guess I just tend towards the normal, and that's okay. The idea of it makes me happy. Do I believe in everything my priest tells me when we have our marriage counselling meetings? No, of course not. But I do think there's something wonderful about partnership. I also think, for other people, there's something wonderful about polyamory. It takes all sorts.'

Marriage is deemed as a socially responsible thing to do, but a responsible answer is not 'it makes me happy' or 'I think there's something wonderful about partnership'. Not that I disagree, but it feels strange to me to make a decision – a lifelong, until death do us part decision – because you like it, or think it's wonderful. Surely the responsible thing to do is ask questions of everything and find structurally sound answers. And openness seems like a responsible, intellectual plundering of the status quo, of received wisdom: the pursuit of happier-ness and of pleasure. Perhaps I'm too harsh a critic of normality. Perhaps for some people that is their pursuit of happiness, of pleasure. It is for Holly.

But it just seems so small, so circumscribed and preordained: something decreed by the Inventor of Marriage years and years ago that we all just sign up to without question. It literally is the age-old adage – if all your friends jumped off a cliff, would you do it too? – but for adults. I'm getting married, and we're staying monogamous, because it's what I've been told to do, it's how someone decided it would be best to organise society. Everyone pairs off and nobody's left alone. So why not make that couples of eight? If a fork had been named a tree we would always call it a tree, and if a marriage had always comprised of eight people who could fuck whoever they want, perhaps I'd be making a case for partnership: perhaps monogamy would be the radical choice.

So who decided then? The first recorded marriage uniting one woman and one man is recorded in 2350 BCE, in Mesopotamia. Before that, it's believed that families consisted of loosely organised units of a few male leaders, and a bunch of women shared between them. That's also not ideal, frankly, but it is a different kind of normal. Then as we shifted to become an agricultural people, marriage became about property, land and the insurance that a father would be legally bound to his heirs.

I can see how sexual openness would be fairly doable – you just have to believe that at the end of all the fucking, you're the one they want to come home to. It's not so hard to grasp, especially when you consider how very few one-night stands you genuinely catch feelings for. In my case, for example, it's none – unless it's feelings of remorse. I can't imagine having sex with someone else and finding it more appealing, or my feelings for them more overwhelming, than those I have for Ace. And I must admit that the idea of sexual openness makes my worries about the finality of marriage dissolve somewhat.

But the idea of being allowed to fall in love with other people is daunting to me. I think, perhaps, that emotional monogamy can be a very non-normative form of care, too, in a world that can feel so uncaring – especially towards those of us who are different. Monogamy means you're committed to loving someone, to giving your time and your energy to another. That feels radical in a world that is burning. Yet monogamy simultaneously feels so boring, especially when you meet such rad people as Amir, Ebony, Cris, Cathy. Talking to them, it's easy to see every choice you've made as something boring, normal, anodyne. But I do believe it: that in a world of people so self-obsessed, it's wonderful to offer that care and love and devotion to one other.

I want to ask Ebony if not having sex makes it easier, but I don't for fear that I might offend her. I think it might, but that's from my limited, overtly sexualised viewpoint. I want to ask Amir if he's ever been hurt by Stan, or vice versa. I want to ask Cris if they ever want to divorce one of their three partners and what it would look like practically if they did. But I don't. Because not being inside those scenarios means there's a certain degree of nuance I'll never be able to grasp, and I'm scared they'll all think I'm simplifying or missing the point of their experiences ... or that I'm an idiot.

5

Ghosts

'I KNOW THAT I'M not insane – I can logically understand why I did it,' a strong Northern Irish accent crackles down the phone. 'It was real to me – and it was part of my life that ended. I never physically saw him, I never physically heard him. It was all done through mental mediumship.'

In July 2016, on a boat in the middle of the Atlantic Ocean, Amanda Teague married a ghost. And not just any ghost. A 500-year-old Haitian pirate ghost, who she says inspired the character of Captain Jack Sparrow in the *Pirates of the Caribbean* movies. I'd tracked her down off the back of the media ruckus her marriage had made when she first announced she'd tied the knot with an invisible spouse, and then, later, 'filed' for divorce (an exorcism, but we'll get to that). Like anyone who pokes their head above the parapet, Amanda was mocked, intensely, for her mystical marriage by disbelievers and naysayers. People called her crazy, sad, stupid, lonely, loony. Yet she also had people reach out to her to tell her she wasn't alone, to tell her that they, too, were in relationships with ghosts.

A real ghost, or a figment of her imagination? The jury's still out on that one: Amanda, to this day, wonders whether she made it all up or whether there was an actual paranormal partner holed up inside her head. But at the time, in Amanda's reality, he was really real, he was there, he was her husband. There were no extenuating personal circumstances, no huge upheavals. She had fallen in love with an invisible man.

When I got her on the phone, Amanda was of course not, as she had been described by many commenters, a lunatic. She was, as might be expected however, completely fascinating. Not because of her link with the other worlds, her orgasms induced by an apparition (only when she concentrated real hard) or her claim that said spectre had tried to kill her. But because of her aspirations to normality. Because she wanted to stick to society's plan too. 'Part of it was just wanting to have a big day, like most women. I wanted to have my big white dress and I wanted to have my party.'

'Posthumous marriage is where you can technically marry your partner after they have died. You know, I suppose for inheritance purposes, or if you were pregnant or whatever. Spiritual marriage is where you are marrying a kind of abstract spirit, shall we say – who you may never have met, or who lived hundreds of years ago. A god or a goddess, that kind of idea.' That's what Amanda's marriage to Captain Sparrow had been – a spiritual one, conducted entirely in her head.

In practice, their relationship played out like most married couples: they fought, they fucked, she did all the housework, she got bored of him and eventually he hurt her, and so they got divorced. 'So I actually had an exorcism in December of 2018. That's how it ended. Spiritually, shall we say. Now I just call myself a widow,' she laughs, knowingly.

I'd first read about Amanda a few years ago when I saw the news on Facebook, most likely shared by my very opinionated Auntie Joan who likes to take a pop at most people on the net (nobody's safe from the wrath of Joan, least of all Amanda). I remember the headline being something along the lines of 'Woman who marries ghost wants a divorce after claiming he tried to kill her'. As is the gay way, I instantly took a screenshot of the page and posted it to my Instagram stories – declaring this woman an absolute icon.

And the truth is, she is. I'd be lying if I didn't admit that my praise of Amanda back then wasn't partly to do with the fact that she sounded completely bonkers. But like most gay icons, in my eyes, she was inherently linked to a kind of indescribable tragedy: in this case, one in which you marry a ghost who tries to kill you. The way Amanda's story was framed by the press made it sound like lunacy and also a deep rejection of normality, the kind of lunacy and deep rejection of normality gays thrive off, and see themselves reflected in. Ergo, icon!

But as you can't judge a sandwich by the bread alone, my judgements about Amanda were wrong. She, of course, isn't bonkers (and that, as I've learned since, is a horrendous word to use to describe anyone). In fact, she's incredibly insightful: someone who is completely aware of how her marriage made her look to the world, and yet aware, too, of why she chose to share her experience so publicly and with such vulnerability. Because while the rest of us keep our ghosts neatly hidden behind a pristine veneer, Amanda married hers.

This vulnerability is another way Amanda's marriage was similar to so many marriages both historically and in the present day. Vulnerability, for most of history, has formed the backbone of marriage – the trading chip used to seal deals offering women protection in return for their servitude. Marriage historians and feminists have both compared marriage structures of yore to gender-based enslavement. For many, this is a reality that continues today around the world, with an estimated 15 million people across the world in forced marriages that, according to the International Labour Organisation, are a contemporary form of enslavement.

From an early age we create ideals because that's what we're told to do: we're told to find the perfect partner and to build the perfect future, following very specific guidelines laid for us by society. Meaning that once we're at the age where this plan becomes action, like clockwork we spend years agonising over finding the person who fits us just right – who matches the plan we'd made so eagerly in our teenage bedrooms – and then when they eventually come along, they never really do.

Not because the people you're choosing are totally shit (I mean, some of them are) but because there is texture to their realities. But we continue to project onto our partners, to hold out hope that the fictitious other half we dreamed of when we were young will manifest in the one we've found in real life. Countless relationships fall apart because both parties involved can't change into the thing the other really wants. And the ones that remain standing, remain completely imperfect. The countless times we've all sat with friends whose relationships seem stunning, while behind closed doors they're harbouring resentments, not fucking enough, working on their exit strategies, or are just plain miserable and unable to leave for fear of messing up their prescribed life plan. We live eternally with the ghost of what we'd imagined and, if we're lucky, we settle for someone almost as good.

Perhaps, I wonder, marriage and monogamy are synonymous with settling for something almost as good as the unknown alternative. Settling down, settling for the person who doesn't ever quite meet your needs. The poly and open people I spoke with had found the practical antidote to that: they had realised that one person, as the old adage goes, can never give you everything you want. That's just the truth of it. What you do with that truth – whether you live with the ghost, or accept what you can't change, is one of life's many battles.

And the battle is a ubiquitous one. According to data from Dana Adam Shapiro's book *You Can Be Right (Or You Can Be Married)* apparently only 17 per cent of people he polled claimed to be happily married. That means there's 83 per cent of us living with a ghost.

Meanwhile, in 2018 'The Happiness Index: Love and Relationships in America' commissioned by eHarmony (lol, branded research), shows that 64 per cent of Americans are 'very happy' in their marriages and partnerships. Of course, this is a study commissioned by a matchmaking website, so by power of deduction let's meet right in-between Shapiro and eHarmony's studies and say that 40.5 per cent of married couples are happy. When you think how many of us end up married, and how that partnership forms the structural basis for your whole life, it's still quite a distressing idea that over half of us are unhappy.

Declaring this social system as one which we must all assume is a given from the moment we pop out as babies – Judith Butler says some brilliant things about how the moment we assign a baby a girl we are in fact inscribing her with a destiny toward marriage – it seems we will be decreed social pariahs, failures, or, like Amanda, lunatics, if we don't engage with the concept of marriage, or if we choose to do so in the wrong way. Moreover, it seems that a lot of people are gonna choose to be unhappy over being unmarried. That we're going to choose to make our friends, kids, families unhappy just because we think they should get married. As Jane Austen wrote in *Pride and Prejudice*, 'happiness in marriage is entirely a matter of chance.' So why do we give our lives over to chance?

Up until 1991 (yes, actual 1991) in the UK, and 1993 in all fifty states of the USA, marital rape was still legal. Christian vows (which started to be used in around 1549) and are still used widely today, would see a woman promise to 'love, cherish and obey' a man, while the man would promise to 'love, cherish and worship' his wife. I smell injustice. Until an economic feminism as we know it became entrenched in western society – let's say the late 1980s when it started to be more socially accepted that a woman might don a power suit, make her own money and have her own ambitions outside of the home – marital relationships promised a woman protection via means of income and housing in exchange for her domestic labour. An unfair trade, exploitation disguised as protection, rendering the woman completely vulnerable to the will of her man. Now of course there are exceptions, but generally so much of the way we formulate contemporary ideas of relationships is built on this trade-off of vulnerability for protection. That's why there's such pressure on people to get married: because historically if you as a woman were left out of marriage, you were left out of society, with no money, and depreciating value as your biological clock ticked on. That's why there were so many gay antigay-marriage groups: because by being barred from a system we could see the system for what it was: boring, Christian, outmoded, exploitative, pressurised and based on the opposite of what gay liberation movements across the world fought for: freedom! Or as Sylvia Rivera put it in 1973, 'What the fuck's wrong with you all? Think about that! I do not believe in a revolution. I believe in the Gay Power.'

Amanda is a fascinating case study of just how much the invisible chokehold of social pressure can affect our decisions, and the very fabric of our realities. 'I suppose, you know, if you dig a little bit deeper, you know like from my generation, I'm forty-seven, you're brought up with this idea that you need a plus-one and pretty much when I was growing up, you had to get married. You know, and you're not really thought of as a normal, natural, functioning person if you don't have this. I was brought up with this idea: if you have this day and you have all your friends there, it's like a validation. Like actually I have got a husband. He might be dead. But I've got one.'

I'm so surprised by Amanda's answer to my question (why get married?) – I'd assumed it had been for the press, for the fun, for the story or even for the love. But no. It was because social pressure on women of a certain age to get married is so strong that Amanda felt less shame marrying an invisible spirit she'd never even seen than not getting married at all. Indeed, Amanda had grown up in an Irish Catholic family who had prized marriage over most things. That's the part which is most absurd about this whole set-up: not the actual act of marrying Captain Jack, but the social pressure surrounding marriage which pervades even relationships as unconventional as those between a woman and a ghost.

Sure, if you scroll through the comments sections on all the articles which talk about Amanda's unconventional marriage, some of the most commonly used phrases are 'delusional' and 'unnatural'. But isn't all marriage delusional and unnatural at its very core? The psychological idea of being legally recognised as a couple, a partnership, is a falsehood in actual reality. Arguably, monogamy might be something inherently natural to some, not all, people; but monogamy and marriage are two completely different things, love and the state are two completely different things, human relationships and their regulation by law are not synonymous. One is felt, one is created in order to control.

But they've become so smushed into one, and we think it is so natural to marry your monogamous partner, that people might go so far as to marry a spirit in order to avoid being deemed unnatural or unfulfilled. When you're seeking marriage you're seeking a universal recognition not otherwise afforded you if you're single or polyamorous, for instance: you are claiming your right to enter the hospital when your partner is sick, you are claiming your right to a shared child, you are claiming your right to cross borders, you are claiming your right to social acceptance, you are claiming your right to forever. But can an unmarried couple not have this? Legally, no – there are horrific stories of people not being allowed into hospitals to visit their dying life partners because there's no legal recognition of their partnership; there are stories of unmarried parents losing children because they had no legal right to see them after the relationship ended; there are stories of the supposedly best couples ever breaking up because one wanted marriage – which has become synonymous with wanting forever – and one did not, though perhaps they wanted forever too.

'Even though there's lots of proof that it really was real, part of me wonders if it was my head making it all up to fulfil this idea that in order to be a whole person, a whole woman, a fulfilled woman, I had to be married,' Amanda said. I told her, 'whether it was real or not, your marriage and your connection with this spirit was as true as any typical physical marriage – and either way it's your truth.' She seemed touched by that.

I'd expected to get on the phone with Amanda and have to stifle my laughter, but our conversation was much more earnest than expected. She told me how she doesn't regret her marriage – even though it ended in so much pain, and caused her father disappointment and friction with her mother – because in the end it helped her realise she is actually asexual. 'And so I'd found a relationship that worked for me on a physical level, and I realised after it was over that I'm not interested in touch from another person.' It was a necessary process, then, for Amanda to end up where she needed to be.

It remains worrying, to say the least, that a person has to go through that: adhere to societal norms so intensely, then be mocked, internationally, for doing just what society told her to, all so she could reach a place where she could comfortably come out as what she always knew she was. 'Being openly asexual in my town, when I was younger, was something more shameful than marrying a ghost I'd say. They'd have thought I was insane.' It's all so ironic, and desperately painful too. That we as a culture have placed so much shame onto women – culturally, religiously, socially – that they must marry at the cost of appearing sane. It's no surprise: the most deified women in popular culture are those who became nothing more than goo-goo-eyed brides: Kate Middleton, Bridget Jones, Carrie Bradshaw. Hell, the world even forgave Jade Goody's racism on her wedding day, and Kim and Kanye's marriage photo is one of the most googled images in history. Meghan Markle, however, is vilified because she seems like an unfit wife, both in terms of her race, her work, her attitude, for a royal; and Princess Diana – once the most beloved bride of all – lost her life because she dissented from the system.

Much like homosexuals are only allowed makeover shows, women are only really ever allowed wedding shows. We may not even realise it, she may not even realise it, but so often our strong protagonists are searching for a man. On a local scale, I know the feeling Amanda is talking about, I've felt it, I've seen it with my own eyes. My specifically working-class friends over twenty-five desperately panicked about ending up a dreaded spinster, so they grab the nearest man to them and marry to tick the box, rather than for actual happiness. Sure, a lot of them are happy – posting images online of cosy nights in and the ring sparkling beneath fairy lights hung in gardens of houses they've bought together. But a part of me wonders if they could be happier. And because I'm incredibly feminine and northern working-class, patterns of gender therein box me into the role of a woman in so many ways, it's expected that I, too, should dream of a wedding. And nothing confirms that quite like when I go home and we get rosé-pissed and I tell them cheekily that I think I want to marry Ace and they all squeal like a chorus of brusque northern angels.

One of my closest friends from Lancaster, who is getting married next year, is engaged to a gay man – he's not out, but he's told her he's gay, or perhaps bisexual, but he doesn't want to be. And so they continue full steam ahead with their day-to-day wedding planning, plugging the volcano that is his repressed sexuality and her repressed want to be wanted. They don't talk about it, because she wants to get married, and he wants to be a heterosexual, and so they will be wed in March, and both of them will live with the ghost of what they really wanted until they die or the marriage ends.

This is the pressure Amanda felt: to concede, to fit in. It terrifies me to think of the number of people who have given into pressure created for them by some unknown system, that those people never question that pressure either. That's not to say there aren't happily married couples, couples who love each other and just wanted to shout it in front of everyone they know. But it's hard to think of a single couple who got married and didn't do it because of some social pressure: religion, parents, tax, children or simply because it's 'what we do'. I think about my sister – who is happily unmarried with two children. The amount of glances, side-eyes, questions about if/when/whether she's going to get married – even from me – are unbearable. And this practice – this cross-examination of those who choose not to have a typically 'normal' life – whether it's a poly person, my sister, or Amanda and her ghost – compounds the pressure put on us by our history, our society, our culture, and creates extreme inequality both in legal terms and in terms of the licenses granted (or not) to the married and the unmarried.

Someone who has spent a lot of time thinking about this – the abolishment of marriage in favour of a marriage-free state – is Dr Clare Chambers. A professor of political philosophy at Cambridge University, her book *Against Marriage* argues for the detonation of marriage in favour of egalitarian equality.

The first thing I'm interested in asking her about when we speak is what we lose in a society which centres marriage. When we talk about marriage it's always in terms of what we gain: a ring, a life partner, that red Magimix you've been dreaming of since you were a small baby. You gain status, prestige, a place in the 'plus-ones' club' as Amanda calls it.

'I guess things are lost, and things are gained, right?' she says. 'I suppose what is lost is a sense of diversity of ways that people can arrange their lives and their relationships. And without diversity, what you also lose is a sense of equality and an openness to change.' It's true: what marriage offers us is a road map for our lives. But what that road map fails to recognise are all the other potential routes – of openness, polyamory, self-love, multiple relationships which give us multiple things throughout our lives – rather than just the one lane we must be in forever. And because straying from that map looks far scarier than sticking to it, many of us are never even given the opportunity to imagine what another life might look like. We are, from a very early age, blinkered and trundling up the well-paved path to nuptials.

'Marriage creates a model of a relationship, a "successful relationship", that we all have to follow,' says Chambers.

'And it also obscures the extent to which that is mostly very messy. The way that we think of marriages as not only being the ideal, but the normal way that people should live their life, doesn't actually correspond to the reality.'

There are those ghosts again – the falsehoods we're taught to believe to be true until we marry and find out they are not. Relationships are far messier than the system might have us believe: it's frankly inhuman to think that we can commit to one person and have no feelings for others, no desire for something else, no longing for the touch of another or a want to just tear our life apart and run away to Seville with that colleague who has the big bulge, and patronises us in a hot way.

Our minds and our desires are messy. But we are told marriage is not. We are told marriage is simple: it's supposed to be the answer to all our longing for love, it's supposed to provide stability. In fact, the very act of marriage declares your messiness over: we have settled down, we are no longer in service for sex or mistakes or the gritty texture of real-life relationships. When we marry we tell the world we are no longer desirable, and we no longer have desire for others. When we marry we tell the world what our life will look like: normal, settled, inside the lines.

Of course for some, this is what they want. Marriage offers us a ritual, a means by which to organise our life, our goals, our expectations and our desires. But imagine, for a second, a world in which that was an option for those who wanted it, sure, but as much legal priority and cultural weight was given to those who felt compelled to imagine something different, felt compelled to veer off the map. Do you think there'd be more love? More understanding? Fewer ghosts?

'We think about things like divorce and separation as failed marriages. So we have this idea not just of a way of life which is marriage, but that that's the only way to succeed,' Clare says. Not to mention being single your whole life, or choosing not to get married at all: those are seen as failures too! 'That shapes the way most of us think of our future and present relationships fundamentally, because either we are wanting to become married, or we're having to struggle with the fact that we failed in that because we failed to find a partner or we separated or something went wrong. Or: we're having to very explicitly and overtly reject and rebel against marriage and live our lives in a kind of conscious rejection of an ideal. It demands a reaction from all of us. We either have to accept it or strive towards it, or consciously reject it.'

I find Clare's point here very interesting: that because culturally we centre marriage as one of perhaps three checkpoints in adult life (the other two being house, kids), these signify success, in a largely secular society, in place of any other valuable personal or community-wide rituals. And therein we are forced to have some sort of response to marriage: we live either within it, or in its imprint. A constant state of either being sopped up by normality, or living in rejection of it. This means we lose not only a diversity of relationship types, we lose diversity in imagination, experience and potential.

Beyond what we lose, there is also the case for marriage abolition along the lines that partaking in the system perpetuates injustice. There are the individual kinds of injustice we see in our lives, our relationships and our homes: the main one being division of labour along gendered lines. There's the most obvious one: the maternity leave. According to Sheryl Sandberg's *Lean In*,

43 per cent of highly skilled women leave the workforce for good after having children, and I'm sure that number would be higher if more people could afford to leave work to take care of their children, or if Sheryl gave a second to consider working-class women as part of a valuable statistic. This gendered difference is also state-mandated: in the UK, men get two weeks of paternity leave before they have to go back to work, and women can claim a whole year of paid maternity leave. Of course it's possible to switch this dynamic around, but in a 2019 report by EMW Law only a third of new fathers actually take any paternity leave at all. The USA is one of only five countries that doesn't mandate maternity pay (wild) and so in both countries and both cases the labour of raising a child will by and large fall to the woman, if possible, given the cost of childcare, social ideologies that say women belong in the home, and the wild disparity in pay according to gender. It goes without saying that this has a knock-on effect when it comes to career progression: in the UK only 27.8 per cent of women find themselves in full- or part-time work three years after child birth, compared with 90 per cent of men.

Then of course you have the house-bound, domestic labour: nappy-changing, feeding, cleaning, caring, cook-ing, all the hours of invisible, unpaid toil that occur within the home justified by the fact the man is the one working (read: making money), which implies that the woman is not. And sure, after the entry of fourth-wave feminism into the mass cultural psyche and onto the T-shirts of hypocritical men everywhere, we hear of examples where 'he actually changes the nappies', or 'he actually split maternity with me' or 'he actually does the washing-up'.

These examples are by no means good enough, and also remain the exception to the rule. By congratulating men for doing the bare minimum, we completely accept that women should take on domestic labour without question or complaint.

I've never seen this more clearly than when I go home to Lancaster. Among my northern friends who are parents, this is compounded perhaps more intensely by the fact that the childcare is undertaken by grandmothers and, to be fair, grandfathers who are retired, with most of the women I know going back to work soon after having a child so that with both parents earning, the family can make ends meet. Even so, the working mother will also take on the lion's share of child-raising and domestic labour. He might do the odd thing around the house – often laundry. For some reason hot working-class men love the smell of clean washing and will often be super particular about it. Don't know why, but there's probably a book in that.

This unfair division of labour doesn't exist only among heterosexual couples. In my personal experience, it often falls along gendered lines within queer or homosexual relationships too. In my case, I am the more typically feminine in my relationship and so I often end up doing things like cooking, washing, cleaning more willingly than Ace. Caveat here to say that, of course, neither of us believe that the feminine should be equated with these things, but it's interesting/distressing to see how subliminal cultural wiring creeps in. The difference in our relationship however is that we've built a vernacular where these frustrations can be expressed, and often by using the schematics of structural gender-based oppression to explain why it's not okay that I do most of the washing, or not okay that he always fetches me things from all over the house once I've taken my seat on the couch for the night.

This is wildly different from the ways I saw my mum manage the household. She and my dad worked full-time, in very stressful jobs, with four kids, and she continued to organise the distribution of chores in the house: each day, leaving an intricate list of tasks for the kids and my dad to complete. And while we were doing the hoovering, the washing, unloading the dishwasher – usually in the five minutes before she got home from work – it's not like we had had to think about what needed doing. And so in this case, her thoughtfulness became work, work that she'd always had to do. Praise must go to my father here, too, however, as his job was intensely stressful and underpaid; and he never once complained nor demanded applause for supporting us or my mother in this labour. But the division is still there: if Mum stops thinking about what needs doing, who thinks in her place?

So it could be fair to say that a lot of marriages, and relationships, are founded on the basis of inequality of labour. This then goes back to the idea that a state which prioritises marriage is a state that dupes us all into caring for each other so that it doesn't have to care for us. When we are married we are taken care of – whether financially or physically or emotionally – but when a relationship so often revolves around jobs, this leaves very little room for joy. What if the women I know, and so many of us know, didn't have to expend their energies thinking five steps ahead, writing job lists, or doing the jobs. What if the men I know didn't have to suffer, often in silence, under the pressure of having to a provide for a family that they never really imagined wanting. What if we were given the space to imagine what we actually want, rather than what we're told to want? So a culture that centres marriage also commits an injustice to its people's imaginations, and to people's everyday existences. There's no way my mum wanted to write a list of fucking chores every day. But she did, because she was told to.

Then, of course, there's the case for marriage abolishment on the grounds that its existence perpetuates structural injustice between those who marry and those who can't. 'There's a worry that in marrying, a person might be benefiting from injustice,' Clare adds. 'And I think that should have really concerned all marrying people particularly before same-sex marriage. I do think that when you are living in a society, which permits marriage only between different sex couples traditionally construed, then if you buy into that system, you are participating in, and benefiting from, injustice – and that's a real problem.'

Consider now that same sex marriage is legal in only twenty-nine countries around the world. Arguably we could be deemed to be implicating ourselves, whether gay-marrying or not, in injustice by marrying – until same-sex marriages are recognised everywhere. Moreover, until marriage is inclusive of various formulations of relationships, then those of us who marry continue to benefit from injustice: from being allowed into a system that keeps others out. From having more rights than our single or unmarried peers.

'You have to remember that refusing to get married to your partner could also mean you're benefiting from injustice. Marriage protects the vulnerable, right, if it works properly. And a relatively frequent scenario is a man who refuses to marry his female partner and can thereby deny her various sorts of financial security they might have should they be married. It's not always the case to say, "oh, getting married means you're benefiting from injustice, and not getting married means you're doing the right thing." It depends on the power differentials between the people involved.'

There are times, of course, when marriage is incredibly useful, too: 'if you have migration status which is uncertain. Situations to do with children, inheritance tax, pension rights. There's various situations where it might be absolutely the right thing for an individual person to marry,' Chambers concedes.

It's an important feeling to reckon with: one which reminds us that a single ideology applied as if society, both nationally and globally, is a monolith fails the very people for whom our politic is supposed to fight.

What about queer people? I ask. Clare's argument against marriage is one that dissects the system, the structure, and not actually the individual who is grappling with it. It looks at all the ways state regulation of our relationships limit our options and remove protections from people both within the system, and without it. I rephrase my question: in a world without marriage, who would take care of the queers: the ones who couldn't get visitation rights to a sick partner in hospital, or the ones who were not allowed access to their dead partners' wills because of family intervention. Who, in the new world order, would protect them and their already fragile rights? I feel smug thinking I might have got the better of her.

'I doubt that in situations where people are denied visitation rights, it's because they haven't brought their marriage certificate with them, right? It's not actually about certification, and definitely about a much more pervasive discriminatory structure. When you're thinking about things like hospital visitation rights, you're talking about who has the power to deny access.' There's an example in *Against Marriage* of a lesbian couple, she tells me, who have just married but are facing exclusion from their families because of prejudice. 'So the point being that the marriage is not helping that, the discrimination is coming socially with or without the legality. The problem is in thinking that marriage is the solution to the problem. It's only a partial solution at best, for those people who have got married. It doesn't necessarily do enough. Not necessarily anything, actually, but certainly not enough to undermine the prejudices and discrimination, which is what caused the problem in the first place. You've got to find a solution that works at a much more fundamental level. Social change.'

Damn. She's right. But we knew that already. So it turns out that there's not really a just way to get married (bar for visa purposes). And that idea of social change should not only be applied to gay marriage – it should be applied to all marriage. Nobody should be seeking legal recognition of partnership to gain protection from the state, because the state's job is to protect us: whether we're single, coupled, or quintupled. So why do we do it? With all this injustice in evidence, why do I still not feel convinced that marriage is something worth entirely trashing?

The sociologist Andrew Cherlin uses the word 'prestige' to describe what we gain from marriage. This is a super smart word to describe the feeling we all get when a friend gets married, and kind of changes. You know, when you're the only one of your friends not even considering marriage and everyone looks at you over a glass of rosé in the pub in Lancaster with eyes that scream 'you don't get it yet, but you will when you eventually join us, O Stupid, Lonely Singleton.' And this idea of prestige only serves to compound the cultural idea that unmarrieds, cohabiters, singletons, are lonelier than their married counterparts. There's lots of conflicting studies on this: in one 1998 study in the *Sociological Perspectives* journal, conducted across seventeen countries, there was a correlation between being married and being less lonely (although in the same study it turned out that men report less loneliness, women more – and loneliness for both parties rises hugely after having children). In 2016, psychologist Bella DePaulo sifted through 814 studies and found that single people feel more connected to family and friends than their married counterparts. What this means, in practice, is that statistically marriage weakens social links to others around you: whether it's to your mum, your mates, or your sister's kids. These studies discovered that those who are married are less likely to visit or call friends and relatives, and, as a result, are less likely to offer and receive emotional support often proffered by these relationships.

According to the same studies, single people, and those who cohabit but are unmarried, are more connected to local communities, more in touch with friends and families, and more likely to care for friends and relatives who are ailing or ageing; albeit these markers are higher for the former category (single people) than the latter (those who cohabit). A prime example of this kind of fluid family is found among my community, the famous 'queer family' so many of us proudly exist within. Cultural representations of this kind of family can be found in documentaries like *Paris is Burning*, the TV series *Pose*, and even in predominantly white shows like *Looking* or *Will & Grace*. Drag families and big community clubs and parties that are attended by the same set of faces, most of whom know or know of each other, exist because in a queer community the need for family – when we are forced out of the traditional idea of it – is urgent. Most contemporary writings about queer families are attached to the HIV and AIDS pandemic which raged through our community throughout the '80s, but other examples – Wilde's green carnations, the iconic communes of 1970s gay and lesbian London, activist groups and drag troupes, showgirls of the wartime era – stretch back further than the ethnographers of our community often mention. In the 1970s, aforementioned queer activists Sylvia Rivera and Marsha P. Johnson founded STAR – Street Transvestite Action Revolutionaries – both a movement and home to care for trans women in America who had been forced onto the street. And before that there are examples of homosexuality and gender non-conformity in every part of the world, and you can bet that with those different understandings of relationships came different ways of being together from those we understand to be the norm today. We as a community have, since our inception (ergo forever), formulated different boundaries of relationships, and countless ways to express committed and uncommitted love.

This is because, unlike your run-of-the-mill heterosexual, our original family ties are often fractured because those who bore us often can't cope with who we are. Society, until recently at least, didn't recognise our relationships as real, and, until a little less recently (I mean, the 1970s here in the UK and USA) our identities, genders and sexualities weren't legally recognised either – so instead we looked to each other to validate ourselves. We became each other's mothers, fathers, siblings, children in the absence of the 'real' or 'biological' thing. Whatever biology means. We have forever been a beaming example of what a world could look like without marriage, because we weren't allowed it – and that world was, and is, differently troubled, complicated, empty and full all at once: but our conceptions of relationships and their boundaries as queer people are far, far superior, and far more emotionally rich and complex than the heterosexual birth rite of get grown then get married. That's just, literally, stupid.

And speaking of stupid, statistics now say that 61 per cent of cohabiting homosexuals in the USA are married, since the passage of the equal rights bill in 2015 because, despite the fact we have formulated countless fluid ways to have relationships through both need and want, many of us also want in to a system that has rejected us for aeons. Me included. That's the psychology of rejection for you: you want what you can't have, what you've been rejected from, and so you work and work to get it, and then, of course, you fucking take it. Your beach body, your stupidly overpriced house in London, your Big Gay Marriage. Because with marriage also comes prestige. And gays love nothing more than prestige.

This means that through both gay and heterosexual marriage there's a chance we lose these community ties we so proudly created. Which means a lot is lost in a world where there's marriage. When Clare and I discuss what is gained, the primary thing is rights, of course, the secondary thing is ritual, and the tertiary thing is indeed prestige.

So with all our data collected: we've learned that marriage relies on injustice, it limits the imagination, it squishes diversity, it has a gross misogynist history and quite a bleak present, which at best strips us of our social lives and at worst creates legal caveats for modern-day enslavement. Why get married at all? Better still, why live in a marriage system? Why, in any case, does the state need to regulate a largely private part of our lives?

'When I first started writing on marriage, I came from the perspective of feminist critique of the institution, and also an emotional dislike of the institution personally,' Chambers continues. 'And I thought, well, we know that feminism is opposed to marriage, so it would be quite interesting to write a straightforward paper that explains why. 'Course I found that it's complicated and not straightforward. I also found that it was necessary to try to separate the legal, structural aspects of marriage from those personal, social, emotional aspects, because it's too much to deal with it all. And I think generally when we think about social rituals and practices and norms like that, you know, they work to create a sense of community and bonding and reassurance. But they do that precisely by excluding and denigrating non-conformity and that's why it's both soothing, and like you say, an abysmal idea. Because in order to interact with something that has that reassuring emotional role in our life it also has to normalise exclusion.'

Clare's book is about marriage abolishment – about disallowing the state to privilege couples with rights that others can't attain. 'The key issue, the point I'm trying to make with the whole book, is that it's not really about what one individual person or couple does and doesn't do. It's about what the legal and social structures are that make that decision the rational one for people to make. That's where the injustice lies. That people should have to participate in an institution in order get the kind of protection and rights and duties that they ought to have.'

It makes complete sense – to abolish marriage in a very literal sense, in a legal sense, in a justice sense, in a romantic and financial equity kind of sense. But what about feeling? What about Abi and Sam and Sofie and Oonagh and people who actually want all that: the legal in their love? I know they don't actively want to perpetuate injustice, I know, in fact, that they just haven't plumbed its depths. And neither had I, until I started on this quest.

Is there a way to be a part of the system while not losing your autonomy or watching your social circle swiftly contract? I wonder if there are any ways to get married without falling down the traps of the institution. Without creating the inequality which traps people in this pressure cooker, often forcing them to choose between a tempered sense of freedom and adherence to social norms, or a feeling of being a social pariah – god forbid, unmarried over forty. There are single people who yearn to be married, there are married people who yearn for a divorce; there are poly people who yearn to be monogamous, and there are people who marry ghosts and end up exorcising them. There are endless conceptions of marriage, just not all legally recognised. There was the woman who married a snake in India in 2006, in accordance with Hindu ritual, and 2,000 people attended (though the snake, sadly, did not). There's the woman who married a dolphin, the man who married a goat in a public shaming after he was caught copulating with it. There's the absolutely legendary case of Erika who married the Eiffel Tower in 2008 – changing her name to Erika La Tour Eiffel (I'm sorry, but like – what an icon). There's the woman who married the Berlin Wall in 1979. There's a man and a pillow, a man and a car, a man and a rollercoaster, a man and a sex doll.

What's interesting about these examples is that they simultaneously uphold the system of marriage by deeming it necessary in order to officialise people's love for these animals/objects/landmarks, but they also delightfully undermine the very practice of 'traditional' marriage by bastardising the idea that marriage is between two people.

'I actually first came up with the idea of marrying yourself, myself. Or so I thought. And it was when I was researching it that I then realised there was a term for it, sologamy. I didn't realise it was a thing really.'

Two years ago Sophie Tanner married herself. She'd had a bad break-up, and her ex-partner had moved on, but she was getting to a point in her life where people were giving her that look. The 'oh bless you, wish I could stay – but – must dash, hubby needs dinner' look. The 'oh poor you, single again in your mid-thirties' look. The same look that's partially responsible for the aforementioned contraction of married folk's social circles. However, instead of succumbing and rushing into a marriage because she thought she should, because society had primed her to since the moment the midwife pronounced 'it's a girl' on her literal birth day, she decided to marry herself.

'I just thought, what better way to celebrate love than with the wedding. And so that's when I thought of having a cultural ceremony that celebrates self-love as one does romantic love.' What that looked like for Sophie was a big gathering – all her loved ones, friends, (some) family there to celebrate the act of a woman in her thirties committing to the idea of loving herself, before anyone else. There was a flash mob too, but we'll skirt over that because I think they're bad taste incarnate.

But really, Sophie's self-marriage, while being a way to honour herself, was also a means by which to subvert the institution of marriage. She didn't care for the legal side (not that one can legally marry oneself, and god knows how you'd deal with that divorce), but she decided that if people were going to pressure her – be it through pity or societal structure – why not do the very thing the world wants you to, while also flipping them off. 'We have an absence of ritual and ceremony to mark self-development into adulthood,' Sophie explains. 'The only thing we have as adults is marriage and it's like – okay, you're not really considered a full adult until you've gone through the gateway of marriage and settled down and I think that's what everyone strives towards, like a tick box.' There's that pressure again. A pressure to feel like we've achieved something as people, because the government gave us a certificate to show that we had. One can't help but wonder whether marriage would be such a cultural focal point if other things in our lives were celebrated with as much eagerness.

Sologamy as a recorded idea is quite a new one, despite the fact being single has been around forever. Of course there's the brilliant *Sex and the City* episode (Jesus when am I gonna shut up about that?) 'A Woman's Right to Shoes' (feminism!!) where Carrie decides to marry herself in order to seek revenge on her complete arsehole mate because she won't fork out $485 for her stolen Manolos! That's suffrage! There's a tonne of smug articles written by white liberals about the empowering act of marrying yourself, decrying all singles should join the self-married movement. There's the famously self-partnered Emma Watson, and there's even self-marriage packages at IMarriedMe.com in the States. If there's a gap in the market – fill it!

To be frank, I was feeling somewhat cynical when I first started my conversation with Sophie. I think I'd read one too many of those op-eds which declared self-marriage as the answer to modern-day feminism, in which people would say things like 'I'm not saying men are irrelevant, I'm just saying I matter' and 'I don't really bring it up on dates, it's a bit embarrassing' and 'I write affirmations of self-love in lipstick on my mirror every morning'. Yes, that oughta do it! These pieces are frustrating to read because generally they are targeted at women, but also because they generally continue to centre men. Moreover, perhaps it's the working-class brute in me, but I've grown exhausted with the idea of self-love, a kind of mass infliction of toxic-positivity that says if you're not affirming yourself then nobody else ever will, that says if you're not having a Himalayan-salt bath then nobody will ever run one for you. It often feels like the aims of (some of) these self-love movements are to better position you to be loved by somebody else. Which is an entirely contradictory exercise.

Trust me, I know: I spent years dieting, exercising, binging and purging, chucking up McDonald's into bushes, squeezing the loud parts of myself into quiet spaces for only me to appreciate, telling myself I looked 'fabulous' in the mirror every morning – all acts which could be codified as self-love praxes, all acts that were really about changing myself so I would be more attractive to others. I don't want to denigrate those who have successfully managed to practise self-love – I think for many, especially those marginalised, the declarative act of saying I Love Me when the world doesn't, is a radical one. Perhaps I have grown tired of the co-option of self-love praxes by those who don't really need it. Perhaps I have grown tired of capitalism.

Plus, it's impossible to be constantly in love with yourself. As legend tells us, we will eventually fall in the lake! And what's more, it's okay not to always be self-loving. Because sometimes we do things wrong; sometimes we should feel bad about sending a bitchy text about someone to the someone rather than to the person who just said a way worse thing about them on a different chat. I don't love vast parts of myself, and while I do love other parts of myself, oftentimes self-love decrees I should love all my 'flaws'. I agree that I should work to value the things in me that society might deem to be flaws – being fat is a real killer example of that – but I don't think I'm without fault, and I don't think I should forgive myself for all my failures. A healthier self-love practice would be one that concedes this, and sees active work and change as something which denotes loving yourself.

So this is not to say that some self love, or perhaps a healthier term is self-work, is not required to survive in a world that makes you feel bad about yourself to sell you things – marriage included – but self-love in a kind of middle-class, white person navel-gazing 'I use a rose quartz egg to balance my energies because wellness and I ignore the fact that crystal miners die every year searching for my ambient energy stones' way is just another insipid, insidious form of people doing things to pass the time because they've got nothing else to worry about. It's white people in the west ransacking other parts of the world and bastardising ritual/practice/resources to furnish the temple of their true religion: the self. All while selling us more shit. And so yes, I'd gone into this conversation feeling a little cynical, to say the least.

But Sophie's sologamous marriage was not about incessantly declaring love for herself. It was more about committing to value yourself, working hard to work on yourself. Realising that a partner is not what you need to live a fulfilled life, to be natural. Sophie didn't marry herself, to work on herself, to undergo an impossible self-betterment phase, so that someone else might notice; she married herself because her relationship with herself, as is true of all of us, is the longest one in her life.

'It's very personal and unique to the individual. I think you could possibly marry yourself just in a very private ceremony on your own. But since I've done it, I feel like a whole load has been lifted off me, because I don't feel like half a person anymore in the same way that you're made to feel when you're single. There's so much pressure put on you, telling you that you're lacking, that you need to get off your butt and try and change your situation. So I feel like all of that has just flown away since I did it. And I feel like I am duty-bound to practise what I preach. And so I go back to my vows quite a lot: face your disappointments, embrace your hopes, those sorts of things. You know, every now and then I ask, am I facing that properly? Often, I'm not. So I'm like, okay, I need to do this. In this relationship, I do feel like I learn every day.'

Sologamy, or perhaps a sologamist marriage, to be more accurate, lies at the strange intersection of conformity and difference. Sophie is at once acknowledging, and arguably giving in to, the pressure put on her to be anything but 'single' in the unmarried sense. And in the same breath, she's undermining the practice of marriage, rendering it somewhat pointless by deciding she can just do it herself. All the papers, all the protections and all the power given to married couples, are flouted by pulling something from the institution and contorting it into another thing that suits you, which, unlike many marriages, actually improves your real life. In Sophie's case, it's something which relieves the pressure she feels, while giving her active reason to work on supporting herself in meaningful ways. And it means that she can better support others in her life. This goes back to the statistics that married people's social lives and circles of care often contract after they've done the deed and signed the deed. Sophie, by marrying herself, has made a commitment to be there for herself, and, in doing so, continue to be there for others.

It's an attractive idea. Perhaps I've just been sucked in by the self-love craze over the course of my chat with Sophie (my god I'm fickle), but if I've learned anything by dissolving into the middle classes, here in my shared studio-live-ex-office in Forest Hill, London, it's that sometimes the emotional stoicism we are taught as working-class people isn't always the best approach. Don't get me wrong, there are self-obsessed working-class people, too, but there are many more self-obsessed middle-class people. And while self-love is not synonymous with self-obsession, a lot of the middle-class people I know have renamed the latter the former and use it to justify bad or thoughtless behaviour.

But in the same breath, sometimes you do need to think about yourself. My upbringing taught me to keep my emotional matters behind a closed door, to ignore the want to talk about my problems or worries because it's worse to lose face than to show people the expression of pain on it. And, as my grandma always said when I huffed at the idea of finishing my peas or complained about not being allowed an unnecessary brand-new garment: 'there are people who have it much worse than you.' But just as I've seen middle-class people stifled by their own self-work – tying themselves up in knots about their ethics, and yet still centring their own experiences – I've seen working class people stifled by their own pain and emotional repression: stuck in unhappiness because sharing the reasons for it might make them appear weak, or self-indulgent. In my experience a mix of both is what works best (although try telling my brilliantly stoic mum that). A dash of the emotionally ice-cold helps when crying about it will do you no good, and a dash of the self-reflection when there's some work to be done to unpick bias or repression when looking at yourself, or at the unequal way you've been taught to move in the world is useful too. As ever, it's a little non-binary.

Naturally, Sophie's decision to self-marry brought with it a bit of a press storm – some good, some bad. But, much as with Amanda, worse were the comments sections (aren't they always) – where men sounded off that this was feminist poppycock, while women attacked Sophie because it seemed as though her actions were actively criticising their choices.

I find it interesting that a structure like marriage, which is so embedded in our society, is something that can't handle criticism. Or more accurately, that the people who believe in marriage can't take criticism of it. But, as is often the case, those who are the most protective of, sensitive about, innovations to the status quo are so inclined because they know the status quo is flawed. And nothing belies this more than a bunch of absolutely fuming Carls and Karens on the old Twit, or the *Guardian* comment section, calling Sophie some truly horrific names all because she did something they had nothing to do with. Methinks the married folk doth protest too much. But if your worldview, or your marriage, can't take questioning then frankly it isn't structurally sound – and that's the issue with those like Amanda and Sophie, or that woman who married a snake, or when Tracey Emin married a stone in her back garden in France (such a shame she's a Tory) – it's not the act that's so shocking, it's the fact that the act calls into question other people's life choices. And those other people, instead of asking themselves why they're so excruciatingly furious about it, spew savage hate anonymously rather than looking at their own actions or, perhaps, inaction, in upholding this system of injustice without actually thinking twice about it.

Solo-marriage isn't going to topple the institution of marriage; and the fight for an egalitarian marriage-free state is a long way away, down a rocky road. Systems exist both legally but also culturally, in our DNA from birth. And while marriages of yore certainly had different formulations, the cultural idea of marriage is millennia-old. Safe to say that to unpick marriage from our psyches – both individually and internationally – is quite a radical proposition.

And, while I'm aware I'm writing a whole book about marriage, there are systems which need dismantling far more urgently, before we get to that of marriage: capitalism, racism, police, prisons, J. K. Rowling.

Sophie presents a step towards that toppling of marriage however – because her marriage wasn't encased in the legalities a usual marriage is usually encased within. There is no legal requirement to protect yourself from yourself (although tell me that when I'm in a bar and I've just been paid an £87.50 invoice). Sophie likes this, and deems it as important as any legal marriage.

And this is where the nefarious clutches of marriage lie: the legalities. Not the ceremony, or the act of committing to someone: there aren't many people, even marriage-abolitionists, who don't believe in love. But it's about deregulating state control of the private. It's about creating a world where your love or commitment to another isn't mired in injustice. Clare Chambers said that to marry as a heterosexual couple before gay/bi marriage was legalised was perpetuating injustice. If you extend that logic to the quadruplet in the previous chapter, who can't have their love recognised, or Sophie who can't have it recognised when she's married to herself, nor Amanda when married to a ghost, then you quickly realise that anyone who is legally married is upholding a state-promoted system of injustice.

We could certainly get into the heinously boring conservative arguments of 'well what about bestiality?', to paraphrase Tory MP James Malliff, and 'what about paedophilia?', to paraphrase every conservative Facebook user ever. For a start, with parental consent it's legal to get married as young as twelve in the state of Massachusetts, thirteen in New Hampshire, and so on, because sometimes the law exists to enshrine and legitimise rape and exploitation, rather than prosecute it; just because something's legal doesn't mean it's moral. But really these moral quandaries which use abstract examples comparing homosexual marriage to bestiality are, to put it articulately, fucked. One is about the denial of humanity, one is about the impossibility of consent. Wouldn't it just be easier to abolish the whole thing altogether so there isn't such moral posturing over something that doesn't concern any other person apart from the two (or more) people involved who, after their super-special day, have to go home and do the goddamn laundry and wipe the crumbs off the goddamn table, and think, god I hate it when he picks a scab and then tries to make it look like he's not eaten it but I can see him eating it?

Indeed, the absolutely reasonable thing, the absolutely just thing – which would allow women to be happier, queers to be queerer, men to endure less social pressure to provide for the family – would be to abolish the whole system of marriage. It would allow us to nurture – like Sophie and Amanda – our relationships with ourselves, and the world. If energy is not created or destroyed, think of the good that could come from all that energy once put into weddings, planning, imagining your perfect future partner for your whole life, now invested into considering the world outside of yourself and outside of your future. Certainly, fewer people would go bankrupt.

This is, of course, naive: it's naive to think that ending marriage might lead us to humanitarian utopia, because the truth is marriage is a fungible system. One that would likely be replaced by a same-but-different system which would continue to replicate the norms created by the hierarchies of power that exist at that time.

There is no solution to social organisation, every single one fails someone, if not swathes of people. And marriage is just a reflection of any social system, like democracy or communism: a failure to so many, while being dressed as a great success in its branding. What we can ask for, what we must ask for, what we must dedicate our energies to, is universal love, justice, equity. That fight will not be won by the overturning of a system like marriage, nor by its inclusion of people once relegated from its protections, but it will be overturned by a seeking of social change, social justice. Then, perhaps, what will arise from demanding more from the state, or upending the state as we know it – and replacing it with a society that values equity, that lifts up those who need it the most – will be less of a need for marriage, less of a need for contracting communities, for unnecessary wedding lists, for pressure. And more space to imagine all the myriad, endless, swirling ways we could love. I have seen this in practice within my community and it is astounding: the care, the accountability, the deep hot want for touch and sex and visibility, alongside the desire and fight for power and justice.

And what about loneliness? Would a world without marriage be a lonelier world? Once again we look to the queer community: where loneliness is often recoded as time to self-reflect, time to learn how to serve yourself and your community better – but it is also actively combated in many ways: by living in communes like Bethnal Rouge, the acid-drag queen collective in east London in the 1970s, or the famed vogue houses from 1980s New York that still survive today. We gather in spaces where we protect ourselves, like clubs, saunas and knitting circles, because the state has never protected us. Of course there's still a material feeling of loneliness in my community. But loneliness will exist with or without marriage. So will romance. And love. And commitment. All of those things are, and have been, the backbone of countless communities not afforded the prestige of marriage. And all of those communities, in my experience, have a much healthier relationship with love, and with reality, than the normative heterosexual equivalent.

'Would you recommend marriage?' I ask my closing question to Dr Chambers. She reflects, 'It's never been part of my argument to say that individual people should not marry. In fact, I've actually advised quite a lot of people to do so, because when you live in a system where significant rights and duties and protections are associated with marriage, there are many situations in which not being married is just really foolish.'

Perhaps it's about asking yourself this question, then: if I were to be married, would I continue to fight for the liberation and protection of those whom the system which I am benefitting from fails? If your answer is yes, then it's better still that we take as many protections from an uncaring state as is possible in the continuing fight towards a different world. So perhaps we should, then. Perhaps we should marry our lovers, our friends, our acquaintances, and gain the rights we deserve already. Because we can be many contradictory things at once – in this case both married and anti-marriage – and we can still believe in, and fight for, a better world.

6

The Business of Dreams

IT'S A LONG-RUNNING JOKE among queer people that there is no such thing as heterosexual culture. That most purely heterosexual culture – when it's not lifted from those who exist outside of sanctioned society and shoehorned into the mainstream like, I dunno, *RuPaul's Drag Race* or sequins – is just mediocre white people doing stuff. Ed Sheeran. Footballers. Keira Knightley.

So nothing could quite prepare me for the day I located its beating heart, the epicentre of heterosexual culture, the mouth of mediocrity: the National Wedding Fair. When I first spied the ad on the tube – two tickets for £25, bridal catwalk, VIP access – I was thrilled. I'd imagined, as I often do when I imagine anything, pure luxury. Hand-beaded gowns by French couturiers, food foraged from the forests of Copenhagen by René Redzepi's nimble hands, music by the Royal Philharmonic whatever it is. This is where all of the impossibly chic brides go to find the best of the best, the premium in Wedding Crap, the perfect toolkit to make your day unique. When I saw the ad – there on the Central Line, the same place I'd seen the 'every second someone in the world gets married' ad some months before – I was feeling good about weddings, about marriage. Like I'd asked some questions and found some answers.

As Clare Chambers says, there's certainly an argument for ditching the system entirely, on a societal and personal level, and sticking to my guns politically. But there's also the reality that I'll likely never have the power to alter the tightly woven social fabric, the one maintained so neatly by marriage, especially when very few people are willing to criticise the system in any meaningful way at all.

Frustratingly, both options feel rather binary, and neither feels totally appealing.

My younger self believed there were no grey areas in life – a sort of outrageous moral judgement based entirely on my own experience – but really, life is completely non-binary. There is absolutely no way to be morally pure across every single decision, or political belief, you have. And so you let the little ones slide: you take the flights across Europe, but try to travel less transatlantically (like I can afford that anyway); you reason that renting is hard, brutal and unstable, so you forgive your once-radical friends who buy houses, hoping that you will one day be able to do the same; you hate capitalism but there's nothing like a pay cheque to quell all of your worries.

There are grey areas. And for me marriage and weddings are that. There's political good: I can be an example of changing convention, as well as showing so many who once thought my lifestyle would lead to my unhappiness, that it's actually quite the opposite. And there's political bad: I would be partaking in a system which isolates and shames single people, or people in poly set-ups; upholding a system which kept me and mine out for hundreds of years; aligning myself with normality, assimilating myself into the same world as 'everyone else'. I would no longer be different.

'How did he propose?' The booking form for the Wedding Fair was a gorgeous role-play exercise to test my no longer being different, because in order to get in you had to be getting married. 'What was the date of the proposal?' I went for tacky and picked Valentine's Day. 'What is the date of the wedding?' The campest date – Halloween the very same year. 'A seven-month engagement,' I fluttered my eyelashes, 'maybe the bride's pregnant!' And budget, from a drop-down list: £1,000,000. And two tickets were mine.

It's bizarre to imagine spending a million on anything, let alone a wedding. Especially when you consider that celeb-wedding culture is actually a fairly recent invention. It was Queen Victoria who should be credited as the mother of weddings as we know them now: white dress, orange blossoms. Charles Dickens wrote to a friend, after attending: 'society is unhinged here by her majesty's marriage, and I am sorry to add that I have fallen hopelessly in love with the Queen.' And the veil continues to blind us, with many of us still seduced by Kate Middleton because she looked great in 2011.

Bursting into our bedroom where Ace was reading, I asked him if he was free on the day. Stupidly, I told him what it was for – 'the National Wedding Fair – we have to go!' – which was my downfall really because, of course, as he squirmed while he scrolled through his calendar, he turned out to be conveniently busy. Something about volunteering for the HIV charity he works for. A terrible excuse. Texted Lei to ask, as he always enjoys switching off his politics and exploring straight culture, but he was working in Paris that weekend photographing some big queer person for the cover of a big queer magazine. I asked three more friends – Hatty was going to a queer rave in Bristol, my flatmate Jacob had a drag gig that night, and my other flatmate Leyah was booked to help their girlfriend lead a workshop in making jesmonite jewellery for the Tate. How stereotypical! I thought – all my queer friends doing their queer things. Shame on them.

At £30,355, the average cost of a wedding in the UK is the highest it's ever been. A quick survey of my girl group from home via WhatsApp, and most of them think – if you can afford it – it's a pretty fair way to spend such money. Although none of them could, to be fair. I ask them why they wouldn't just give the money to a charity. They don't respond. An annoying question from me, to be honest, and one I don't know how I'd answer either. But looking at these figures I was somewhat confused by how a dinner, drinks and a dress can end up costing the same as a down payment on a one-bed ex-council in Peckham.

My assumptions that everything to do with a wedding would be the ultimate display in luxury were surely correct: when the worth of the industry in the UK alone is £10 billion (nothing compared to USA's $72 billion). But really, I would learn very swiftly upon my entry through the breeze-block gates of hell and into the National Wedding Fair, that these statistics don't mean that people spend millions on their weddings; they simply mean that there are a lot of people getting married.

Three weeks later, and I'd completely forgotten about the Wedding Fair after the initial excitement of momentarily believing I was a bride. I was obscenely hungover after drinking almost all of that week's wages at a drag king night in east London. I woke early, to a call from my friend Amrou, who had just got a new Maltipoo puppy – the gayest kind of puppy imaginable – who was in a panic at an early morning emergency vet appointment. 'My puppy's prolapsed,' they yelped down the phone from an echoey clinic, 'I gave him some beef jerky and now he's prolapsed.' The puppy was fine, but the interaction was unforgettable. Both my night and my morning had been very pointedly queer – a drag king band and a prolapsed Maltipoo puppy – but I had to prepare to blend in with the heterosexuals if I was going to succeed at the Wedding Fair. A black trouser, a black jacket and New Rock leather platform boots (these are very gay, but they are the least gay shoes I own save for my Ugg slippers but I couldn't stoop that low).

Now, what's the most shocking thing you've ever seen? I've seen a lot of typically shocking things: the inside of a dead giraffe; a trans performance artist wiping her bum, from which she's just defecated, with pages from US *Vogue* as a comment on the grotesqueries of the fashion industry; I've seen models in gowns fall over on catwalks; and I've seen someone spend a few million euros on one diamond necklace at a private jewellery view in Paris. I've seen my queer friends beaten up, and I've seen them laugh at the trauma. I've seen Coldplay in concert.

Yet despite having watched Chris Martin sing 'Viva La Vida' to a stadium of glow stick-bearing Karens, nothing could quite prepare me for the shock of the National Wedding Fair. There, in that monochrome temple to matrimony, on a particularly hungover Saturday afternoon in Kensington's well-loved exhibition centre, I felt a genuine deep sense of bodily shock at what lay before me as I entered into Heterosexual Pandemonium. I had imagined this would be the opportunity to create a unique day: an all-you-need kit, tailored to you ...

Before I'd walked in, I spent ten minutes on the street outside getting into character – listening to Des'ree 'Kissing You' and Sixpence None the Richer 'Kiss Me' (my two wedding songs, I hate myself), trying to summon forth tears at how beautiful my special day was going to be. If I was going to be talking to wedding vendors I needed to have my story straight. I thought of Ace and all my friends and family in a field somewhere, high on MDMA, dancing to love songs and celebrating not just the happy couple, but all of our love for each other, somehow – with the help of those at the wedding fair – pulling off the perfect, unique, luxurious queer anti-capitalist wedding.

But this was way too queer for here, so I changed the story: my name was Jack, I worked at Deloitte and I was gay but definitely not queer. There, I headed up our LGBT Equalities committee and I didn't think Boy George did anything wrong – and what even was a they? I liked Atlantis Cruises (google it) and I thought Alanis Morissette was punk music (that bit's true, I do, to be fair). My husband-to-be, James, looked like me and we lived in Elephant and Castle and the only reason I was this fat was because I bust my knee at CrossFit six months ago and I hadn't been back since. I liked healthy dinners, long bike rides around London, and getting barebacked in Holiday Inn Vauxhall on a Saturday night while my JJ (my pet

158

name for him), edited it in iMovie, and uploaded it to our XXX Twitter account @hardcorehubbies (iconic!). I voted Tory, but I didn't really like to talk politics (not iconic!).

Even with my homonormative gay mask hiding my true wedding desires, approaching the wedding fair felt like a moment of self-acceptance for me, a wedding-obsessed girl in a radical queer world. I was prepared to sneer at the whole thing, but I was somewhat disarmed by a feeling of self-acceptance. Just like I'd spent all those years in my early twenties accepting parts of myself that seemed unsightly to many – my gayness, non-binaryness, fatness, drag queen-ness – I was accepting another part of me in this moment. The romantic part, the hopeful part, the part that grew up desperately believing love would erase all my feelings of self-hate – and still does. And the part that believes it's completely legitimate to get married and have babies and dream of the perfect day because by god I deserve it. I was liberated just admitting it, aloud: that, actually, after all this moral turmoil, all the smoking and eye-rolling at all the weddings I've been to, I do want it: 'I do want to get married!'

As I neared the convention centre I was jolted from my imaginary wedding day haze and brought back down to earth by a sign that read 'UK VAPER EXPO', with a queue stretching round the block of men in shoes that looked like duvets and bootcut jeans. I swiftly realised I was being really judgemental, and stopped myself; after all – just because vaping hadn't worked for me didn't mean that other people – and by the looks of the queue that was white, heterosexual men – didn't need space to gather and exalt their interests the way I might go to a queer club to watch icons of my community dance on sticky bars. So

I walked on, in the middle of the February storm, and finally reached Olympia West, situated on possibly the greyest street in London.

Like hundreds of enemy mafia families, clusters of predominantly white, predominantly working-class women elbowed each other to get through the door. It dawned on me that the Vaper Expo was for the men, the grooms, and the Wedding Fair was for the women – something which was later confirmed by three different brides I spoke to inside. Icky stat: 98 per cent of all heterosexual weddings are organised by the women, according to the UK Wedding Report. Be a princess for the day, sure, but take on all the labour in making that happen. Hence, I stuck out like a sore thumb – even though I'm not a man, I looked very much like one today (whatever that means). But really these women were no different from me: white, not posh, seeking happiness. I walked up the stairs in a mad bustle of people talking about wedding jewellery and the fact that there's a free Aperol spritz on entry (they don't tell you there's a decade-long queue), and I felt surprisingly comfortable. I felt like I was with my fellow sister-brides and we were about to enter dreamland.

It's impossible to describe what lay before me when we finally got to the top of the carpeted stairs. Imagine if *The Apprentice* met Charlotte from *Sex and the City*'s brain, and then slash the budget twenty-five times. Over a tannoy I could hear pumping drums, on my right women were getting their teeth scanned onto giant screens, a happy-looking dentist telling the crowd that the green parts indicated layers and layers of plaque, with brides-to-be signing up to their mailing list quicker than Britney's wedding to Kevin Federline.

There was a stall called Perfect Tipple which was selling iridescent wine and Sham-pagne in pink, gold and dark blue. I thought for a second that nothing on this earth could make me drink a glass of that, until I was offered a free shot and of course I drank it down with ease. 'Gorgeous!' I told the vendor. In truth it kind of tasted like the smell of my grandma's carpeted bathroom. God rest her. There were jewellers, hair-removal experts, free brow makeovers, gown after gown, string quartets, endless terribly lit wedding photographs, hen and stag organisers, a VIP area that was honestly cordoned off by some pink balloons and I've never wanted to be a VIP less, IKEA (apparently you can flat-pack your wedding now?!?), tiaras, crying mothers of brides, surgery consultation units (dark), a distinct smell across the whole venue of crêpes, and then two men sat in sun loungers in the corner of the room taking pictures of me and laughing. Must be the boots. I felt oddly sorry for them; the joke was really on them. And just like that, my want for a wedding was starting to waver, here in these fiery pits of normality, this petting zoo of heterosexuality.

Free goodies seemed to be the main goal for this section of the fair – and brides and their teams roved around like contestants on Supermarket Sweep, rampantly grabbing anything from fabric samples to a single Velcro roller. It's safe to say that it dawned on me fairly quickly that I was not, in fact, sat snugly in the lap of luxury and instead I'd been hurled into a Pinterest board torn straight from the pages of women's magazine *Red*: with its op-eds about, quote, 'why being nice makes you happy' and cover splashes which read 'RELATIONSHIPS: CAN YOU STAY HAPPY IF YOU STOP HAVING SEX?'

It's so strange: our ubiquitous cultural focus is on having a unique wedding and yet – according to the UK Wedding

Report – 60 per cent of couples attend a wedding fair when preparing for their wedding. That means that 60 per cent of couples who are in the process of planning their unique and special day pluck out their decor, flowers, dress and photographer from the same travelling circus of late-capitalist delights. It seems the wedding industry is selling a false idol, a poorly packaged uniqueness kit. A contradiction in terms, because if everyone's unique, nobody is. Kind of like how Frank Sinatra's 'My Way' is statistically the most popular funeral song: the irony of picking a song about how you did it Your Way when a massive percentage of other people picked the exact same song to declare the exact same thing. It was the same here at the wedding fair: everything has been predetermined for us by The Industry.

Then – a riot broke out. People's faces turned from politely competitive to sheer primal rage: the bridal catwalk was starting and everyone wanted front-row seats. Me included. By the time I'd careened my way through countless bridal parties like a rhino in the problematic film *Jumanji*, I found myself stood, along the back row, watching model brides and grooms traipse down a catwalk in absurdly indistinct outfits while clapping to the music. I looked around and, honestly, everyone was filming the show. Every single person. Again, me included. When a neon sign that read 'Woo' flashed up, and the baying crowd did as they were told, I suddenly snapped out of the reverie.

After the final bride took her bow, the room became a maelstrom of feral bridal parties, as a DJ plugged in and started blaring a bunch of 1990s trance bangers – many of which I'd been dancing to the night before. And, from this foaming crowd which was now flocking to the fake sparkling dance floor in this windowless conference room, in full sincerity there emerged a saxophonist and a bongo player – both engaging in what can only be described as a 'sound-off', playing their instruments while aggressively staring both each other and the crowd down as if in some kind of gladiator funk-off fight to the death. They were both white, and it was the death of music as we all know it, and it was all occurring in front of my now-scarred retinas. People were loving it – joining in, cheering for their winner. Women filmed and men gathered in packs and danced like my lad friends used to dance at sixth-form parties in high school – foot-tapping and finger-pointing. All of them still hampered by the fact that masculinity as we know it deems we must never be seen to dance like we're actually enjoying it. I didn't know what was worse – the men, one of whom was in a CHOOSE LIFE T-shirt, a slogan adopted by ACT UP during the AIDS crisis, monkey-dancing as if to mock the very act of dancing, or the women who were spellbound by this dreamy display of male musical aggression. It was like watching a packet of crisps come to life.

I decide the only thing to do to save myself from either morphing into one of these dancers (indeed my foot was tapping) or screaming like Meryl Streep in season two of *Big Little Lies*, was to flee the building. I tore past brides-to-be, as they dreamed of their dream days. I wanted to tell them that it's all downhill from here – that 'gender will creep in, you know' and 'sure he does his own washing now!' But the last thing anyone wanted to hear was my jaded opinion.

In a talk at Hay Festival in 2019, the economist Paul Dolan said, 'We do have some good longitudinal data following the same people over time, but I am going to do a massive disservice to that science and just say: if you're a man, you should probably get married; if you're a woman, don't bother.' In his book, *Happy Ever After*, in which he uses ATUS (American Time Use Survey) he finds that married men are healthier, happier, and that married women of the same age are less healthy, less happy and likely to die sooner than their single counterparts. Perhaps it's a little dramatic to make the jump, but society is literally asking women to dream of an untimely death. Imagine presenting that statistic to a budding bride as she had the plaque scraped off her teeth. Not today, Satan.

So instead, on my way home, I called Holly.

Did she think she did all the labour? The wedding planning? The cooking? The washing? 'Absolutely fucking not. He does all the housework, and I pay his phone bill because he earns less than me.' Right, sure, but what about kids? What about when they'd have kids and all these great parts of the relationship got thrown in the blender and came out perfectly reordered along gendered lines? What about when he went back to work and Holly had to stay at home with the kids? 'Oh my god Tom, why are you like this? I want to stay at home with the kids. Yeah, sure, some women don't and that's shit, but I can guarantee for a lot of working families spending time with your kids in your house with your dog or whatever is way more appealing. I get to do that, and he doesn't. That's way worse for him.' Sure, Holly's opinion can't be taken as gospel – since there's endless anecdotal and data-based evidence that this is not the case – but it's worth thinking about the other side.

My whole 'men are trash' thing doesn't always hold up when we get down to it. I'd never really thought about it, to be honest – that a lot of people don't love their jobs, or, perhaps more correctly, don't love their jobs more than they love their family. It's all very well saying 'women go to work!', but what if that work is underpaid, long hours, exploitative, or just fucking boring? Lots of women want to return to work, and would much prefer that option to raising a baby, but for some – like Holly – that's not the case. It's not always a simple choice of 'be empowered or don't be empowered' – it's sometimes about choosing the lesser of two evils, and people make that practical choice. So I shouldn't be patronising to those people who are aware of their options, who bop at the Wedding Fair and make a choice as to which is better for them, because all of our choices have been limited by that heady mix of capitalism and gender. Within this world, there are ways to have happy marriages, and maybe it's okay that the thing that signifies this – The Wedding – is the thing people dream about.

So what if people want something different to what I want? I find this hard when it comes to things like politics, or homophobia or racism or takeaways – like, there are simply, fundamentally wrong opinions, sorry to break it to you. But when it comes to something like marriage? The opinionated side of me thinks it's a load of rubbish and agrees with all the stats that prove that women shouldn't get married. But when it comes to the reality? When I talk to my friend Gemma, she tells me that she's 'desperate to get married and take his name' – is that so bad, really? She explains, 'My dad left when I was young, and I just want to feel like part of a family unit. I can't wait.' Here is where weddings become redemption stories, they become more than just a fairy tale: if my background is dysfunctional,

I'm going to pay for a day that broadcasts that my future is pristine.

Another friend from Lancaster – Jade – is fascinating when it comes to her reasons for getting married. 'It's not that I want the big day. But I want the security.' Jade was the product of an affair, and had a completely absent dad. Then her mum met a man and they moved their life from Bolton to Morecambe, and then her new, wonderful adoptive father passed away. Jade was my first girlfriend at school, lol. We laugh about that for a second, and then I ask her why getting married is so important then, if it's not about having the day you dreamed of all your life. 'I want security. After I've had so many men in my life disappear, whether through death or being shit, I want security. I want to know that if something happened to me, or if something happened to Dave, we would be taken care of if we were left alone. You know, legally. Plus I don't have any family left, except my mum, and he has a really big family – the idea of being officially a part of that is something which really excites me. It really makes me feel loved again, in that family type way.'

I tell Jade that I think that's possibly one of the best reasons to get married, and while I don't think she needs to actually tie the knot legally to be included in another family, she tells me that something about it feels more legitimate. Of course, since marriage between a couple is the only type of legal recognition of a relationship in the current system, I agree. The problem isn't Jade, it's that there are no other options.

And even for couples with relationships that don't look at all like Holly's or Jade's, they have the same concerns with family, safety, stability; in fact, when you're queer, these three things are particularly precious and hard to come by. Hatty and her girlfriend Margo are similar, while being completely different. I didn't realise – because they are both so completely anti-establishment – Margo, a trans lesbian Marxist polyamorous icon, Hatty cis but the same – but Hatty revealed to me recently, when I was talking to her about the fact there aren't very many decent reasons to get married, that she and Margo had been thinking about it. 'I think it's important for Margo to feel included in a family. She has a complicated relationship with her own, so for her to feel included in my family would be a huge source of healing and acceptance for someone who's never felt that.' I find this wonderful, and such reasons make me believe in marriage as something which can heal your past traumas because someone is standing up in front of the world, telling you you're loveable; marriage is someone including you in their family – and sure, the 2.4 family is deeply oppressive for many, but perhaps when you haven't had it like Jade, Gemma and Margo haven't, should you be held to a political, ethical standard and judged by me because you just want to feel included in something bigger, in something that so many others have?

So maybe it's okay not to give all the money to charity. Maybe it's okay that the average cost of a wedding is £30,355. Maybe it's okay to go to wedding fairs, and dream of both your day and what your day gives you access to: marriage, security, inclusion, safety, in the only way so many societies know how to provide these things. It's a systemic issue that we don't provide these things for other conceptions of couples – for poly couples like Hatty and Margo, asexual people like Amanda the ghost-loving lady, spinsters and bachelors. That the only recognised type of inclusion in the west exists between a couple, and maybe their family/families.

So, I went home and decided that I was going to get a grip and stop guffawing loudly at all the women on the train who were carrying Wedding Fair totes. I mean, I was too. If I were to watch all my friends get married, I thought perhaps it would be worthwhile to work out what might make a wedding more bearable than all that wedding-fair flat-pack shite, only so I could share any wisdom with anyone who might listen. So I could help make Jade's day better, or yours if you're reading this. If I can't dissuade my marriage-obsessed mates that they deserve more than a fucking day, then I can at least try to make that day as perfect as possible. I can at least help them unclaw their dream days from the nefarious, slimy hands of the Wedding Industry.

Google: world's most expensive wedding planner. Enter Sarah Haywood.

Sarah Haywood deals in dreams. And not iridescent alcohol, wall-to-wall grey carpet dreams. No. Sarah is the ultimate wedding planner, the most premium in all of the world. Her client list spans billionaires, royals, celebs (although this is completely untraceable). She is to weddings what Chanel is to handbags. Lauded by *Vogue* (British and US), friends with JLo, maker of the biggest, most lavish weddings. On her website, when you enter the budget of your special day, there are two options: above a million, below a million. Grotesque, but ever so glam.

Sarah started her career in broadcast news, over twenty years ago. There, she learned how to put a programme together. 'It's much like a live event: you've got a running order, a sequence of events, you've got a budget, you've got to be creative, imaginative,' she explains, when I ask her over Zoom how she became the world's most coveted wedding planner. We were supposed to meet at Annabel's – Mayfair's most elite members' club frequented by everyone from Rita Ora (lol) to Dustin Hoffman – but sadly her schedule was so tightly packed that she called in from her home office.

After the news job, she worked in mid-range weddings for a long time (and by mid-range, I mean the best wedding you or I have ever, or will ever, go to). Then, about five years ago, she realised nobody did the top-tier weddings. The kind of weddings for the kind of people who think the Dorchester ballroom is drab, less glam than their day-to-day life.

'When I first started as a wedding planner, we didn't really know what they were. They had them in America, so I was really lucky to establish a business before wedding planning was even thought of as a career.'

I wonder when the turning point in UK wedding culture was: when we started to believe we needed a wedding planner in order to get married. We see them in films and on TV. I wonder if this is just a thing for the upper echelons of society, the over-moneyed-no-taste set, but upon a quick google I find a bunch of wedding planners who will work with a range of budgets: most notably Shoestring Weddings Thornton-Cleveleys who can do a wedding for under two grand, although after a quick text exchange with them it turns out their business went bust. But online, there are countless ways to do your day cheaply: for under the national average, and way under what Sarah's charging. I think of my friend Anna again who works two minimum-wage jobs and spent £9,000 on her big day. It was an absolute crock of shite by Sarah's standards, but it was probably way more fun than any wedding she's ever created.

'We are born, we get married, we have children,' – after twenty years in the biz, Sarah is quite the life expert – 'then we die. And when you're lying on your deathbed you're thinking about your loved ones, about the most important relationships in your life. And one of them will be the person you married.' Lest we forget Queen Victoria, mother of weddings, was buried in her wedding dress. Grim.

I have a strange soft spot for Sarah – she's a glam laugh-a-minute, and way more self-aware than so many of the posh mums I met through friends of friends, at 21st-birthday parties while I was at university (once I met a mum who was literally nicknamed, I shit you not, 'Bin' in the way that posh people have posh nicknames like Minty or Butter. But Bin, which to me had only ever meant the thing you fill with trash until near overflowing then complain about taking out when your mum asks you, was a step too far). But Sarah isn't like the Bins of the world – she's funny, smart, self-deprecating. Over the course of our conversation she has no qualms about burning some of her previous clients' tastes (although she'll never name a name) while proudly admitting she is, indeed, the best. Like the Miranda Priestly of weddings, after two or three gins. So it slightly disappoints me that her take on marriage, after all these years of watching rich people marry then divorce then marry again then divorce again, of watching well-to-do millennials get married to super-rich baby boomers for the (£) love, that she still believes in marriage.

I'd be lying if I told you I wasn't nervous about meeting her, this big wedding behemoth, but she proved me wrong, winking at me throughout, aware that the weddings she plans are in many ways grotesque: dealing in the world of millionaires, of making dreams come true for those who can afford to dream of anything, is unethical on a human level. £30,000 on a wedding is one thing. But millions is another. As we all know, nobody makes millions – they take it from those who work for them. And such class inequality is only amplified when it comes to what your wedding looks like because your wedding, as I learned at the Wedding Fair, is what your dreams look like. Why should Sarah's clients get solid-gold dance floors and JLo as entertainment while other people get married in a local working men's club and have their nan make their dress? Sure, the latter actually sounds way better, but the inequality still smacks.

'Marriage is the one thing that sets the human species apart from every other species that we share the planet with. We've been doing this in some form since the beginning of recorded time, in all parts of the world independently.' She has a point, although let's not get into subjective realities because wanna bet octopuses think we're all dumb monogamous imbeciles – and don't elephants have funerals (but not weddings ... hmmm ... interesting)? 'Some communities practise plural marriage, others practise very different forms of marriage. But here – where divorce is less stigmatised now than when I first started – we still say "I am going to stick with you. I'm going to stick with you for better or worse, richer or poorer, sickness or in health." That's quite a big commitment.' Yeah, true. 'But you're saying my love for you is this. That we are going to do it, we're in this for the long haul, 'til the end of our lives. And those are the values that we're going to instil in the next generation. It's something that keeps us as a species moving forward.' Yikes! 'It's a boundary that we can work within and we like boundaries. The most successful individuals have boundaries, and marriage is a boundary.'

I guess I shouldn't have expected a radical academic takedown of marriage from the world's premiere wedding planner. While I'm unsure what Sarah means by marriage moving our species forward (from where? to where??), in a way she has a point. A point that chimes with the words of Holly and Gemma, a point, perhaps, which chimes with me: a person searching for the alternative – perhaps in my politics, or my sex, or just the feeling of my day-to-day life as I spiral down this mortal coil, smoking twenty a day until my inevitable early death. I find something so appealing about having boundaries in order to anchor yourself, in having limits in order to work out how to work around them. My queerness is such a perfect example of that. So much of my life has been about rejection of the boundaries set by 'normal' – although I am loathe to say that I as a queer person only exist in light of the heteronormative (and, to paraphrase my fave Judith Butler, it is actually the hets who exist in light of us, because our difference came first, thus allowing them to give name to their normality). I digress.

But yes, I like this idea: this idea of declaring love, commitment, even if it isn't commitment in the way Sarah's rich clients know it, or in the way my mum and dad know it. But if it's commitment so I can go out and a fuck a stranger and then come home and fall asleep next to the person who knows me better than anyone. So I can have my unusual love celebrated in the usual ways. I think of a wedding – not even a Sarah-style wedding, but like a sticky-floored, meat-and-tatty pie in a church hall kind of wedding – to Ace and it makes me feel joyful. I think of everyone who loves us, and everyone who we love, rejoicing in a rare moment where this pair who haven't held hands in public once in a five-year relationship stand up and spout words of adoration and commitment for each other and I'll remember it on my deathbed, even if it goes up in flames.

So I ask Sarah how to make a dream wedding. What do I need – money? Connections? Her?

'The best weddings have two things, trust me: heart, and a consideration for how it feels to be a guest.' I pause for a second to think about how weird people with money are: that people who have infinite money have the prerogative to insist that it's not about the money. It's all very well for Sarah to emphasise 'heart', but it's not heart that makes the guest experience second to none, is it? There's such a bizarre emphasis on discretion among the super-rich: that everything is about money but it's naff if it's that overtly obvious – the same super-rich who would look at a show like *My Big Fat Gypsy Wedding* and think it absolutely grotesque, even though it's the super-rich who got married in giant dresses on TV in the first place.

I ask Sarah how to give a wedding heart, and she doesn't really have a formula; instead she says it's about ensuring the core values of the couple are represented. So she'll spend time trying to get to know them: what they like, what they don't, who they are as people. I imagine this can be quite tricky with the super-rich because greed and tax dodging aren't necessarily things you can put on show at a wedding, but I think Sarah means more like – where do they come from? What does love mean to them? Where did they meet? Why do they love each other? And how can these things, the things at the core of the relationship, be

173

framed and prioritised in every detail: from the location to the place settings, from the floral design to the food.

At Sam and Abi's wedding, they had Polaroids of their guests and little notes about what each person meant to the couple at every place setting; they had food they had both eaten on their first trip to Italy, a place they had grown to adore more than anywhere else; and the tables were named after books they'd both read and argued over. I thought that last one was particularly sweet: because it encompassed the idiosyncrasies of their relationship rather than just 'we once went for a walk in Windermere so this table is called Windermere', because, like, we've all been to Windermere. But the way to make something feel full of heart is to have the details and the specifics considered. Sarah agrees.

The next most important thing about weddings, in Sarah's expert opinion, is making the guests feel cared for. 'We spend a lot of time thinking about what it feels like to be a guest. If it were a one-day event, for example, I would be thinking about that coat check. It's a given that by this point it's going to look stratospherically amazing. But nobody wants to arrive at a wedding and not be able to get through the door because there's a queue to check your coat. And these are things that I think lift the experience from the ordinary to the extraordinary. Now nobody's going to notice that they didn't have to queue for their coat. Nobody's going to say afterwards, "wow – they were so slick at coat check", but they'll notice if they weren't. They aren't going to notice a sparkling washroom, but they'll notice a dirty one. They aren't going to remember a £20,000 centrepiece if their chicken is cold.'

In short, wedding guests are judgemental little bitches. And it's true: we are. My god how many times have we all pursed our lips at a trash speech, the same old rock-covers band, the mason jars, the vintage dress that isn't quite what you'd imagined. What about that dry beef? Purple-and-green-colour scheme? It's a strange culture, really – the whole thing – where we create pressure, where we focus on marriage and find it slightly uncomfortable when someone says they're not doing it, or they're just doing it "us two on a beach somewhere". Where we decree that someone's strange if they don't get married, and yet sit around brutalising the weddings we do go to, smirking about how much better, and how differently, we'd have done it. But that's human nature for you: we love to slag each other off.

Yes, Sarah can make anyone's wildest fantasy into a living reality. A thought which makes me feel both calm, and poor. But it's refreshing to receive advice that none of our cultural depictions of weddings and marriage will give you, because all of them decree that the more dosh you drop, the more memorable your wedding will be. In *Sex and the City*, Carrie's dress (which she's unrealistically gifted by the Last Living Punk, Vivienne Westwood) would cost, in real life, $24,000 (the whole botched wedding, by the way, is estimated to have cost $229,869. I'm screaming). In *Bride Wars*, perhaps the most godawful film since anything Rebel Wilson's been in, Kate Hudson's rock would ring up at about $138,000. And the whole film is predicated on two very successful women who have been friends for years burning their entire existences down to the fact they now hate each other because they booked the same fucking wedding venue on the same fucking day. Jesus. In fact, every possible cultural depiction of a wedding I can think of in recent years reflects the fact that the wedding industry has exploded. But this explosion has given us a kind of economic dysphoria.

Sure, Sarah gets to claim that the only thing that makes a good wedding is altruism: tenderness and heart. But that altruism is a smokescreen for what really makes a good wedding happen – money, and lots of it. Really, what these cultural depictions of lavish weddings with real heart do is use romantic notions of 'kindness' to launder them from the taint of overt spending.

Carrie Bradshaw and the two women in *Bride Wars* are presented as aspirational, but not unusually rich: they're middle-class professional women living in New York City, or so we would believe. So there's this disconnect – screen depictions of middle-class weddings have the aesthetics of Hollywood multimillionaire weddings. And so we bankrupt ourselves.

People love to watch weddings – they love to watch expensive weddings and dream, and they love to watch tasteless weddings and judge. We've all done it, we've all sat there and shaken our head at that poor girl who scarred her hips for life on *My Big Fat Gypsy Wedding* because her dress weighed twice what she did. That we found grotesque, but Carrie? Classy. And in *Bridesmaids* – even though the whole film criticises the growing class divide between two once-best friends – there they stand at the end, in their Fritz Bernaise $800-apiece bridesmaids dresses – while a laser show fires off behind Wilson Phillips (adore) (who have reformed for one night only?). I mean *Sex and the City: The Movie* and *Bridesmaids* might be the best films to watch when you want to switch off completely and roll around in your own hungover filth while eating your ninth Domino's of the week, but the subliminal messaging behind most of the films we enjoy – *Bridget J, 27 Dresses, Four Weddings, My Best Friend's Wedding, My Big Fat Greek Wedding* – are all in some way centred around weddings. And these films that focus on women and female friendship, are made for female audiences. Why is it that representations of weddings and the run-up to weddings are still the storytelling structure we so often reach for first when telling stories about women?

But it turns out we've been duped: you don't need a tonne of money to have the perfect wedding. According to the world's best wedding planner, it just has to reflect you. Whether it's a *Peaky Blinders*-themed wedding (that's what Jade, my first girlfriend, is doing) or a giant cross-generation ceilidh (please don't invite me) it doesn't matter, as long as people feel shrouded in you.

Sustainability is another thing people seem to be increasingly concerned with (and rightfully so). This is something Sarah has been particularly conscious of in recent years, as she started to plan weddings for younger people for whom this is a concern. 'People spend millions with me, on their weddings. And people go on about how obscene that is. But the actual obscenity is the waste. Is how much goes in landfill. The waste from one of my weddings, just one, is probably more waste than I will create the rest of my life.' Sarah goes on to list all the ways in which waste comes into a wedding: the plastic-wrapped flowers, the floral foam, the food packaging, the wedding favours, the carbon footprint of getting it all there. Even if everything is sourced locally – a huge late-capitalist trend – things still come covered in non-recyclable crap. It figures, when the UK wedding industry creates, in a year, the same amount of plastic as 500 people do in their entire lifetimes.

But here is another opportunity to make your wedding a thoughtful occasion: sustainability! And, more importantly, here's how to subtly virtue-signal to everyone exactly how sustainable you're being! For the shallow among us (me) there's no way your critical friends can call you out on a zero-waste wedding, where the cocktails are fashioned out of apple rind from your mam's compost bin, or where the straws are made from straw. And, bingo, you also get to actually do something responsible for the climate, and make people think while in attendance at your wedding, not just sit there and complain that it's not a free bar! Zing! That's manipulative and green! Like my friend who once bought her awful stepfather a donation to a charity for Christmas after he'd been terrible to her: she gets to donate money, and he gets no Christmas present but also can't complain about it. We really do love to see it.

And while indeed Sarah's incorporating sustainability into her weddings, it's not because she's always felt it was morally right, but because a new generation of her clients want her to and will pay for it. The steps she's taken don't benefit the environment: they just offset some of the damage. Of course, a little change can go a long way, but in order to be effective this change needs to be structural – because there are more brides like the ones at the wedding fair, where virtually everything was wrapped in plastic, than Sarah's elite handful of clients. The problem isn't going away.

Removing my gay and cynical lens from the scenario, sustainable weddings are something which will become an increasingly real factor in the future of this growing industry. Shane Connolly is a friend of Sarah's: he's a 'floral alchemist' and he did the flowers for the Royal Wedding. Shane's big thing is sustainability. 'I once did a wedding on February 14th – a cliché – but there was a wall of snowdrops, because they were in season, and everyone got to take a bunch home and plant them in their gardens. That's the thought, the thing that makes people remember the day fondly. Or you can give all the flowers to a great charity?'

'I think that is the role that flowers can play in a wedding,' Shane explains over the phone. He's in his garden, somewhere outside of London, tending passionately to his homegrown beauties. To be frank, I don't think I've ever thought about flowers in my life. But Shane spends all his time thinking about them. 'They can be like a redeeming feature to the whole excess.' Hmmm. 'They can be something that is recycled. Of course, there'll be waste, you know, there always is waste in big events, the caterer can't make thirty chicken breasts, he has to make fifty because somebody might drop some on the floor. But the flowers have just got a potential to give a real, thoughtful message. Because if anything is thoughtful, if you get a thoughtful gift from a friend, it means so much more than the valuable gift. And I think that's the same especially for weddings.'

I think Shane hit the nail on the head there. It's about the thought. To Shane, the flowers reflect that; the intent of having a green wedding. And, really, the thing that unites all bad weddings, when you actually think about it, is the lack of thought. This is what's so disappointing about marriage as a whole, too.

The lack of thought about the very institute, the lack of questioning. Going back to the wedding fair: it's the mindlessness that made me flee. I would have much less judgement for my friends who do get married if they were to ask more questions about why it is they need to get married. But they don't ask questions about the why.

So many questions of what – what will she wear, what will we drink, what will we dance to, where will we honeymoon, the icing: rustic or fucking fondant – but never why. Why do we need to get married to show our commitment to each other? Why do I need my father to give me away? Why am I spending my life savings on a day? Why do I need to feel accepted by a family that's not mine? And why am I giving no regard to the consequences this day will have on the environment? And that's so disappointing. The apex of our very short existence here on earth boiled down to a single day.

I'm exaggerating, as ever, and, really, weddings are mere gateways into married life. And as all the movies really tell us, as all the advice we are offered reiterates at some point: it's about the marriage, not the wedding. But do you really believe that? Because if it were about the marriage, why would we have such elaborate weddings in the first place? Why would my working-class friends be comfortable with spending £30,000 on a wedding? Why would Sarah Haywood's clients come to her and drop millions if the marriage was, really, enough? Perhaps the marriage bit is just a useful moral addendum to make us feel comfortable with the excessive pageantry of weddings.

'Why are you crying?' Ace asks me, with concern, after finding me lying on our bed with bridal brochures spread out around me and Sarah's website up on my laptop screen.

'I'm not crying at pictures of weddings, don't worry. I'm crying because here lies the living depiction of the intense inequality of this world we live in.'

'Tom, come on. Food banks! Homelessness!'

'No, I know. I know. But people who use food banks and people who are homeless have these kinds of dreams too. Those things are real, but being forced to put a tiny budget on your dreams is something which makes my heart feel like it's breaking.'

We talk some more, and I get really angry. Not with him, never with him. But with the world which decrees we must dream about this institution, creates culture which says this must be the start and end of your dreams, and then creates a system wherein you have to do the whole thing on a Shoestring (even though they've gone bust).

Before Victoria's wedding, weddings weren't about fanfare. They were about trade and peace if you were rich, and they were about social roles if you were poor, and they largely happened in people's gardens. Fast forward a hundred and a bit years and now all of our wedding obsessions are compounded by films, magazines, social media. The Industry. We are told what to dream about, and we are told how to dream about it. After finding all these alternative depictions of marriage, the Wedding Fair has left me deeply cold.

'But what else would we dream about?' Holly asks me when I explain why I've been sending her such manic messages over the past few days.

'I don't know,' I respond.

7

The Holy Trinity

THERE ARE SO MANY ways to get married. There are so many different kinds of ceremonies, rich cultural practices, varied religious traditions, all of which have one common goal: to make something out of nothing.

What this something is, of course, means different things to different people. But whatever its meaning, marriage is a nothing which we have made into a something. A something to which we have attached huge emotional meaning; accepted as something unquestionably real; understood as something completely natural; enshrined in the laws and institutions that organise our society. But in fact – much like governments, owning property, Pret – marriage is entirely constructed. Marriage is like having to believe that a plane is flying in order to keep it in the air; we have to believe in marriage for it to exist. Take that belief away, and there's no material, empirical evidence for it.

Looking at the long and dramatic history of the institution, change is perhaps its only constant. As more people have won the right to marry, we've seen vast shifts in the law and changes in religious practices and to the cultural idea of what a marriage is. Indeed, the religious scriptures stay the same, but the ways they are applied and interpreted vary, because in order to achieve the ultimate function of marriage (submission to a higher power by all parties involved) and in order for it to work (mass participation in said submission), marriage, over centuries, needed to ensnare as many people as possible.

This is not a good thing. Having our imaginations of life beyond patriarchal societal structures and beyond a culture that deems marriage to be natural and anything else as unnatural, cleaved from us at an early age means we all lose. It's also not surprising: almost everybody is searching for some sort of higher power to which they can submit. These structures, while they might take a lot of our power, also allow us to find purpose, community, stability, support and understanding. They allow us to find the thing marriage pretends to have: meaning. And, like Holly said, they allow us to dream of something.

Now, it's not very cool to be Christian. Perhaps I speak only for the circles in which I run, but if I'd said a Hail Mary for every time belief in God the Father, Son and Holy Spirit had been grimaced at by a set of cool arty queers around dinner tables in London, I would still be in conversation with the Virgin Mother right now.

White Christianity is what I'm specifically talking about here. Perhaps because among political queer communities, there's an awareness that the white Christian is responsible for the oppression and destruction of countless other faith systems in the world over history; perhaps because white Christianity forms the basis for western society as we know it, and generated the norms that rejected us; or perhaps, simply, because white Christianity is just so lame. Never was there a less alluring aesthetic than an acoustic guitar, a firepit and a non-alcoholic beer.

I grew up fairly devoutly white Christian: believing in its meaning, submitting to its power. Not like the self-chastising monk from *The Da Vinci Code* – a true corker of a movie, if, like me, you enjoy watching culture being swallowed into a big budget black hole – but a young person who believed in God because that's what we did in the nineties and noughties in the north. There was no other realm of thought beyond it, and while it didn't dictate my life in many of the ways devotion does for others, just like it rained, and we knew rain was natural, there was God and we knew God was natural. It wasn't really up for discussion. Of course, eventually, when I'd speak to my mother about this many years after I left home, she would remind me that we never talked about God because neither she nor my dad really believed in any of it. But, belief or not, we were culturally entrenched in the Church.

My grandma was a Methodist, my mum a lapsed Anglican, and my high school Catholic. Religion was a daily constant: prayer, Bible study, group worship and confirmation classes.

Now, a Catholic education is not as scary as it sounds. Sadly there were very few smells and bells, and obeisance to the laws of our Lord and our Church was stretched rather thin: just ask the pair from my school who were caught shagging in chapel, or twelve-year-old me who got sent out of Sunday service for laughing hysterically when my friend Mark taught me slang words for vagina as the congregation sang 'All Things Bright and Beautiful'. It didn't overrun our lives, but religion was something we did often and interrogated rarely. Much the same way we do marriage. As it would happen, one of the things that was a given in our Christian education was that marriage would be one of the key steps on your journey to heaven (not the gay club).

Until I read *Secret Diary of a Call Girl* at the age of eighteen, while burning to a crisp on a sun lounger on a girly holiday to Benidorm, where we stayed in the premiere uno-star extravaganza, the Grand Casino Royale, the Bible was the book I was by far most familiar with. I assumed that everyone was like me, that everyone knew the Bible inside out – since it formed much of the moral compass of supposedly British values, and since even the most morally corrupt member of my girl group could tell you the rough plot. So when I got to university and met people who didn't know what the Shroud of Turin was, I was opened up to the idea that maybe God and rain weren't the same.

University was the first time I'd had a choice as to whether to go to church or not. Growing up it's not like we hadn't had a choice, it's more that the choice had never been presented to us. And going to church was an important part of our community, and nourishing your reputation within that community. It was what you did, and it was how you accrued points both literally (to get you into school) and figuratively (so your neighbours wouldn't think you were depraved).

This attitude threads through the life of so many people who grew up religious. That Church was as much about scoring points with people as it is about scoring points with God. And this attitude threads through into our ideas of what a wedding, and a marriage, looks like. That a wedding and a marriage are an instrument of whatever God(s) you worship, and that a marriage outside of your religion's church holds less meaning – and won't be seen as legitimate in the eyes of the religious community, neighbours and friends you grew up with.

It was through my grandma Kathleen I learned the importance of nourishing your reputation. Much like I will show my face at queer clubs in London, to support the community and also remind people I exist, Kathleen would apply make-up, set her hair, fasten her one set of pearls, slide her cracked heels into a pair of Gerry Weber mules, and put on her posh voice for church every Sunday without fail. Church was Grandma's queer club.

When I finally reached a queer club of my own, I denounced my religious upbringing, and the path it had me on towards my natural progression into marriage. Not publicly – it would be too embarrassing to admit I'd been a choir boy in Lancaster -- but privately. I'd sat around and agreed while we talked about Richard Dawkins, and I'd bitched about the girl in my year at university who duped me into going to a conversion class at a church just outside of town. For some reason an eighteen-year-old me had had the wherewithal to get up and leave. Perhaps it's because I had been aware of my gayness for so long, and sat with it in church on a Sunday for many years, that I was one of the lucky ones who realised I hadn't yet burst into flames. Perhaps even more fortuitously for me, I had read the Bible liberally and realised that God loves everyone – even faggy little me who was, by the age of fifteen, taking dicks in the bum in a mint-green Corsa parked outside a gym in Morecambe after revising for my RE GCSE.

I still feel uncomfortable with the concept of atheism. I still feel a sort of numinous pull towards the life path of a Christian – because it's hard to rewire the ways we were built as teenagers and it's alluring to imagine, even for a second, that if God really does exist it might well be possible to please him. That, if God really does exist, you could have access to something so natural – something that created the natural – that you could be connected to something far larger than it's possible to fathom.

Marriage creates a similar kind of connection. One which allows you entry into a way of life respected by countless people both alive and dead. You aren't cast out alone like Moses before he found that burning bush, or Muhammed as he meditated on Mount Hira. You are connected to the past, to legacy, to the choices made by others in your community. And that connection to a higher structure creates the kind of meaning most of us are desperately searching for. The same one I found in queer dance parties, the same one my grandma found at Church.

And the search for meaning is terminal. Everybody does it: whether you're the kind of wanker who says all religious people are stupid and loves William Burroughs, or the kind who uses religion to justify homophobic hatred, everyone clings to meaning.

The Bible emphasises marriage in such a way: the words husband and wife literally appear in the Ten Commandments, and from the very beginning of the book the meaning of this union is both held with utmost reverence and never, ever questioned. The Bible, the Quran, the Vedas, the Torah, the Guru Granth Sahib all have slightly differing attitudes to marriage, but all of them say that it is essential to marry in order to live a full religious life. It would be stupid to imagine that my religious upbringing hasn't been an influencing factor on my desire to get married; I've been so conditioned that I think of marriage not just as a natural and normal thing to do, but a morally righteous one. Not that I'd consciously judge someone living with a partner they're not married to – but on some subconscious level the prejudice is there. I value marriage in the way my religion taught me to.

Ace is an atheist. A devout worshipper of no God. Of death meaning, to quote him, 'eternal oblivion' and religion being at best a collective purpose, and at worst a means of control. Our differing attitudes to God is something that has never really come up unless we're drunk in a particularly chatty corner of a house party and we start to earnestly unpick the meaning of life in the way all middle-class 'creatives' do once they've finished talking about the *Guardian* front page. It's not our fault: Whispering Angel is a truth serum! And despite hours of droning chat about the universe expanding into nothing, and it all being too perfect for there not to be a God, I always end up saying I'm agnostic, while he says he's atheist, and that's it.

Perhaps this would be different if one of us were devout, committed to a God so much so that that commitment might shape the way we want to live our future. But since he's an atheist, and since I live a distinctly un-Christian life, imagining raising children in the church, or getting married because my once-unquestioned faith tells me to do so, seems like something that's not worth getting my old choir robe in a twist about when it comes to our relationship.

Our value systems are very similar – something that has fared well for us when we're debating an ethical issue, a political issue, or even where to go for dinner. We, most often, empower each other in our opinions, or challenge the other when one of us is wrong. This is quite frictionless usually, both of us aware that we receive our information and our ongoing educations about the world from various sources – and there's a generous understanding between us that partnership does not mean sameness. It means we both have subjectivities that cause us to approach certain ethical issues, political issues, or restaurant choices differently.

That said, his often-cavalier disregard for the idea of God is something which, if I'm honest, irks me. 'I find it arrogant that you think your belief system is something which trumps everyone else's,' I'll say, 'and I find it terrifying that you think this whole thing ends in eternal oblivion.'

'What do you think it ends in: heaven?'

No. Not necessarily. Maybe. Either way, conversations of faith can often make even the kindest people into judgemental arseholes. Not that Ace is ever an arsehole, but when it comes to questions of value systems often the problems we're presented with earlier in our lives – uni, lying about whose house you're sleeping over at, getting bum-fingered in a bush – are less based on value systems than those that meet us later in life like marriage, kids, The Big Life Stuff.

For Saavi and James – these conversations are going to be tough. 'My family's from Sri Lanka, and they're Hindu, and James's family are from England originally, and are Church of England.'

Saavi and James had three weddings. A legal one, a Christian one and a Hindu one. Each one had varying numbers of guests, and both partners felt technically 'married' at different times. 'For me, I certainly felt more married after the Hindu ceremony, and I reckon James felt more married after the Christian ceremony.'

It's all pretty simple, and conversion was a no, on both sides. In fact, Saavi explains that it was wonderful to celebrate both of their cultures respectively to which I reply: 'there's no such thing as white Christian culture.' She doesn't laugh.

'To be honest, it was just a given that we would have a religious ceremony. I don't think we ever discussed not having one. Not because either of us are particularly devout per se, even though James is certainly interested in Christianity, but because we are culturally religious, and because our parents are religious. But the weddings were easy – they were fun, and we got to have more than one. When it comes to raising kids together ... I guess that's when there'll be more complicated conversations that have to happen.'

Interfaith marriages happen all the time, and are rising in number due most likely to increased global movement and loosening ties to religion. In a 2015 study, the Pew Research Centre found that while almost 70 per cent of married Americans say their spouse shared their same religion, nearly four in ten Americans who have married since 2010 claim to have a spouse who is in a different religious group. Interfaith relationships are actually super common between those who are unmarried – with 49 per cent of surveyed Americans living with someone of a different faith. That's a lot of faith!

I wonder if being in an interfaith marriage causes Saavi any strain. Sometimes the biggest fights I've had with Ace have been about faith, even though neither of us care that much about it, nor would we link ourselves to any religion. But that's booze for you!

'Well, James is strongly like "I will want my children to go to church and understand Christian values." I'm probably more like, I'd want them to appreciate Hindu culture and values, but I don't know if I would push for them to go to the temple. Maybe once a month. But then if you think about it from a kid's point of view, is that not quite confusing? So I don't know what we'll do in the future.'

'Someone must always compromise, at some stage,' explains Nameela who was married to an atheist, and since then has divorced. 'I found myself becoming a more devout Muslim when I had my first child, and that was something that my ex-husband said he hadn't signed up for. Certainly there was a cultural pressure from my family to ensure the child grew up in the Islamic faith, but at the same time there was a cultural pressure from his white family to make sure, I don't know, their grandchild wasn't lost entirely to Islam. But my ex-husband was an atheist, so there was no conflict of schedule when I wanted to take our child to mosque. And he seemed to blame me for my beliefs; but his beliefs, or lack thereof, were the obstructive ones. It's easier now.'

Much like Nameela's departure from her husband, hindsight makes my departure from God seem like a no-brainer, something that required no thought, and something that will in no way affect my life going forward.

But this is perhaps the first time I've ever sat down to think about it. To think about how I still feel a jerk of shame if I do something considered particularly sinful – like watching aggressive porn, or saying something unnecessarily bitchy about someone who definitely doesn't deserve it. I still pray before a flight because I'm terrified of dying in a plane crash, and all the way through university I spoke to God every night before I went to sleep, asking him, in a very naive way, to bless every living thing on earth in a prayer I had learned, and loved, in confirmation group. It's interesting to speak to Saavi and Nameela – both whom were not particularly concerned by how much their faith might affect their marriages at the time of their wedding. But Ace is an atheist, and while I'm no church-goer aren't these questions that must be confronted before you arrive at the altar?

When I think about marriage, or about not getting married more specifically, I often wonder if that will disappoint God. That's Catholicism for you: a niggle of guilt. A question mark where an obvious answer should be. Part of my distancing myself from organised religion was certainly because of those question marks. Could I be a gay Catholic? Could I be a cohabiting Catholic? Could I be a slutty-bottom-pig-who-loves-daddies-and-golden-showers Catholic? I don't think so. And so it was easier to answer the questions for myself, and understand that I would sooner change the Catholic part of the question than the slutty-bottom-pig-who-loves-daddies-and-golden-showers part. And really, not because I had a pro-gay priest growing up, the answer to me was clear: that my relationship with God, if any, was one that was for me and not for Catholicism as a whole.

193

So I made peace with the parts of myself that didn't fit my denomination, and slowly I lost touch with that cheeky little Lamb of God. And yet still some of the questions – the ones I didn't need to answer when I was a gay eighteen-year-old walking out of Conversion class in my thigh-high pink Converse boots – still need answering today. Now I'm here, talking to married people, and I'm asking new questions of my religion from back then. Of course I dealt with the questions that arose in my early twenties during my first ecclesiastical emancipation – the gay stuff, the drag stuff. Most of my moral lines, I am loathe to admit it, are drawn on the black-and-white lines of Christianity, so it wasn't too hard to imagine how making a home porno with a colleague in Hong Kong didn't go against the Ten Commandments because, thank God, it wasn't mentioned in the Commandments. Of course, I have other friends who have left religions for whom the process was an incredibly long, complicated and drawn-out one. I have a friend who still feels angels on their shoulders totting up good and bad deeds because that's what they were taught in Islamic class at a young age; a friend's auntie has converted to Judaism, Christianity and Islam for different marriages; I have a friend who is bisexual, and who was a Mormon, and got married to a woman to work out which path to take.

Meet Zach.

'I mean, if you want to commit to each other and say that you're going to try to be together forever then fine. I don't really know what the value is in being like, I'm going to be with you forever no matter what. I think it makes more sense to be like, I'm just going to work on something until that no longer makes sense to me. I don't understand why you would commit to making anything work no matter what.'

Zach is an old friend of mine. When we first met at university, he was perhaps one of the more interesting people knocking about, among an array of upper-class white women who somehow managed to have endless financial resources and still complain about everything. Zach, however, rarely complained. He was always so funny, warm and sensitive, and it wasn't until I really got to know him that I learned more about his path in and out of Mormonism.

'In Mormonism you're supposed to pray on things until you know it's true. You're told to pray to know if the Book of Mormon is true, pray to know if John Smith was a prophet. But really what you're actually being told to do is to pray until you know that John Smith was a prophet, pray until you know that the Book of Mormon is true. And so you're just, and this might not be the exact right term, gaslighting yourself because you're like, "that is what must be true and therefore if it's not working the problem is with me". And so if this marriage must work no matter what, and it's not, then the problem is with me. And not with the marriage.'

It wasn't until after university, some five years later, that Zach announced his marriage to a woman on Facebook. I knew he was a Mormon, but I'd always thought he was into guys. Perhaps that's just because I fancied him, or perhaps because he'd always been so uniquely kind for a cis man. (Not that all gays are kind.)

Perhaps he always seemed so perceptive because he was forever asking questions of his own beliefs. In fact, he'd asked so many questions and only found more questions where he was told answers should be, that he decided to get married to see if there were any answers there for him. It was an ethical situation in many ways: in that his then-wife certainly knew that Zach had questions both about his faith and his sexuality. As he tells me with candour, he'd been a perfect Mormon in terms of following the rules: and so by the time he was twenty-six and getting married he'd never sworn, masturbated, had sex or drunk alcohol. This marriage, in many ways, was his parting shot: one where he and his partner could safely explore the expanses of desire and intimacy and still follow the rules.

'So just before I was married I was on my way out of being religious, and my relationship was one of the last vestiges of my religious life, and probably only happened because of my religious life,' Zach tells me over a coffee in the forecourt of a cinema in central London. He's so hot, it's hard to concentrate. 'So I had accepted myself as a bisexual, but I didn't really know what was going on, although I knew there was something confusing. And I knew I needed to do something about it. So I just thought, when my [now] ex-wife proposed: "Oh, actually, you know, we're really connected." This was an opportunity to explore sexuality within the boundaries of what my religious confines would let me do. And then if it all went pear-shaped, I would just deal with that then. That, obviously, was silly, in retrospect.'

Zach and his wife divorced a few years ago and he, with that decision, officially left the Mormon faith, while she stayed. He'd been a missionary, and a devout Mormon, until his sexuality had led him to ask questions of the things he'd believed to be true growing up. I try to tell him that everyone seems to get married for silly reasons or, in fact, reasons that aren't reasons at all. 'Perhaps,'

I wager, 'your reason for getting married is one of the few legitimate ones: to ask questions and find answers, rather than to just follow unblinkingly.' He smiles.

'Definitely being working class, black, and especially being bisexual, massively makes you question Mormonism, which is something that fetishises a middle-class, nuclear family lifestyle. What people are striving towards [in the Mormon faith] is success in their career, beauty in their bodies and a strong relationship.' Is that not the central aspiration of all white, western society too?

'If you're gay the most straightforward way to be a Mormon is just to be celibate. But if you live in a more liberal area, and you're willing to just accept that there will be all of these, like, religious sanctions, but maybe not social sanctions, because let's say you're living in Massachusetts, or let's say you're going to church in central London, then that is fine, too, but you just have to be prepared to live with constant aggravation.'

Zach codes his decision to get married as a mistake because when he left it he then came out. That's not to say he doesn't have a powerful friendship and connection to his ex-wife. But much like me, Zach felt his faith and his sexuality couldn't quite tessellate. There's this age-old adage in the gay community – that religion is a choice but sexuality is not. But cases like Zach's make me wonder whether religion is really a choice. It's certainly not a simple one, one that we are aware of. Rain is rain, until it's not. And trying to tell people who believe rain is rain that you no longer do is a process that's just as hard as coming out: because leaving behind a belief system is so often synonymous with sacrificing large parts of your cultural and social make-up. And Zach's all too aware of that – so much so that he made a choice to get married before he made a choice to leave his religion, and all the connectedness it afforded him.

This connectedness is powerful and important. It's why we all put our faith in structures. But sometimes the gains we make from our religions – whether the queer community or the Mormon church – can blind us to the pressures we concede to in order to grasp onto the gains.

'So, in Mormonism, there's two kinds of things that happen to you if you've lived a perfect life, let's say, or like perfect enough to be cleansed in the Atonement of Christ. So, if you are single you can achieve salvation. And you essentially become an angel for eternity that serves God. And if you are married, you achieve exaltation, and you achieve godhood. And you can't achieve godhood without being married. So everyone wants their children to achieve godhood. And in Mormonism, there's like all of these like folkloric things attributed to Brigham Young. A terrible human anyway. But a quote attributed to him is: "an unmarried man over the age of twenty-five is a menace". It's so culturally produced that it's such a pressure on people to get married. I got married so late as a Mormon. And, like, a lot of women, for example, don't celebrate their twenty-fifth birthday because it's a time of real sadness. There's just so much pressure.'

Indeed, many of us might not attribute this pressure to faith, but these faith systems are perhaps the largest informant of the moral codes of so many societies in which marriage remains the central organising principle (even where religion is seemingly not present).

And even where marriage is not the centre – like in my queer community – there's other types of pressures. Pressures to do the opposite, pressures to resist structures, pressures to not assimilate and pressures to not even crave that assimilation. If marriage affords you godhood in Mormonism, radical polyamory affords you godhood in the queer community.

These pressures are nobody's fault per se, or no single person or religion's creation, but while God might have given us free will, society has taken it, twisted it, and made it hard to comprehend what free will really is.

So Zach had decided not to 'rock the boat'. To use marriage as a kind of trial to test his waning relationship to his religion before he left it behind entirely.

'My ex-wife was still a Mormon, even when I had stopped going to church. I was in this weird middle space. I was Mormon but not Mormon. I kept following Mormon rules for like two years after I stopped being Mormon. I went to church for ages when I didn't believe, and when I stopped going to church, I still didn't drink, I didn't swear, I didn't do loads of things. Now I'm so not Mormon.'

Zach has a unique perspective that many of my peers don't. Sure he's a young divorcé – which I tell him is actually very chic, very Joan Collins, and he laughs – but how many people in their late twenties can say they've learned fundamental truths about the landscape of life? That they've asked questions many people won't ask until they're thirty years into a marriage, or that they might never think to ask at all?

'I mean, I think going through this has given me so much certainty in where I am now, whereas maybe had I not been through this I might still be on a quest. Like, there's no part of me that even thinks for a second I might be Mormon again, or there might be validity to these ideas. Maybe it was the only way I could learn that. But I kind of like to hope that it wouldn't have been the only way ... because as good as some of the things were, and you know, me and my ex-wife are still friends and all the rest of it, there was a lot of pain. And it became a toxic dynamic, and, like, surely nothing is worth that. But at the same time the things that I've learned, the ways that I've grown, are perhaps the biggest leaps that I've ever made. And I'm really glad that I've done those things.'

When he first announced his intent to get married to a woman a lot of Zach's non-religious friends thought it wasn't the right thing to do. Not because they were necessarily concerned about Zach, but because they thought that (while proclaiming to be liberal) the sacred system of marriage could not be treated in such a way.

'Basically, a lot of people who are not religious seem to think that because they're not religious their lives are actually very secular. But like, your life is actually very religious. Yeah, you have grown up with this liberalism that you haven't even interrogated, but at the root of it are Christian ideals. And when I was telling people about getting married and viewing it as a trial, it was my non-religious friends who were like "you can't do that", "that's not a marriage". My religious friend were much more understanding, in the hope that this might tether me back to Mormonism.'

'Maybe it's a healthier way to view marriage,' I respond. Zach's journey through marriage and his faith was incredibly complicated for him, but it's also arguably been a more productive experience in comparison to the ways many of us get married – and continue to stay within difficult marriages, because of its supposed sanctity – without asking any questions. Zach's marriage was the opposite, it was full of questions: perhaps brought about by being at the intersect of faith, sexuality and commitment, which gave him the tools to ask more questions. And while indeed this produced pain and a toxic dynamic for Zach and his ex-wife, many marriages where no questions are ever asked produce years of pain and hideously toxic dynamics. They just perhaps don't show themselves in the same way.

'I had an old Catholic aunt in Nigeria. She died two years ago. And her husband treated her terribly through her entire life. Like, she probably died in her late fifties from cancer, and he beat her over her entire life. And on her deathbed, my sister was with her and she was basically crying out, saying "my entire life I've loved my husband, and all he's ever done is treat me badly. I've suffered, and I tried to be good, to stay with my husband" and mid-sentence she died. Like literally mid-sentence, crying about the fact that her husband treated her so badly, her entire life, and the only reason she stayed with him was because she thought that that was what she was supposed to do. And I'm like, why, why, why? And that's what marriage does. Because if you think this thing must work at all costs, and it's not working, just do more, just put in more effort, do something else, find another way, find a way to soften your husband's heart, be patient. If that's marriage, then I don't know if I necessarily agree with marriage at all. Because sometimes the problem is just not you.'

Zach had accepted that the problem wasn't him, so he got divorced. 'I never actually wanted to get married. I used to say to my mom when I was younger, "I just want to be alone." I don't think there's anything wrong with that. But Mormonism is not about that. When you come back from being a missionary, marriage is the next thing you're supposed to be focusing on. And then I stopped being Mormon, but it's still really hard when the purpose

201

of relationships in my religion are that they should lead to marriage. And so to suddenly not think of that thing, that that's the point of a relationship, is hard. You can't just enjoy a relationship for the sake of enjoying somebody's company. It's like: is this person going to make a good life partner? Do they have the qualities that are going to make them a good spouse? But I think the main reason I got married was so I just wouldn't have to decide at the time whether I was going to actually come out fully. And start, like, living.'

Now Zach is out, and he doesn't practice Mormonism anymore. When I ask him what it was like to get divorced, he said it was 'the most powerful I have ever felt in my life. Because I felt like I was taking back control.'

And so perhaps that's what matters: feeling in control, being controlled. Perhaps many of us who are religious are seeking to add a layer of control onto a life that needs it, a life that can feel unbounded; and perhaps that control doesn't work for others and so they find other social codes to adhere to. It's the same with marriage – it controls, and it's controlled, the parameters are understood and so we create confines in our lives – much like commandments – that set out clear pathways of how we should live. Because then it's easier, then the responsibility stops beyond you and your partner, and is attributed to this big thing in the sky – God, or the state – that has told you what to do. Much like marriage is used by the law to control society, religion also uses marriage to control and organise the world. So our individual search for control takes part in a bigger, more systemic structure of control.

Of course it's naive to boil thousands of years of religion down to it all being a mechanism of control, and of course many people find both freedom and comfort in their faith – the way I do it in my queerness. But aren't we all seeking systems of control: not God, or the state, but queer politics perhaps; fluidity, perhaps; celibacy, perhaps. To find something outside of ourselves which can bring purpose to our lives – for which there is seemingly no real purpose at all.

In my early twenties, when I was discovering drugs, dank online hook-ups and direct-action activism, I thought these things were papering over my childhood obsession with church weddings. Now I realise I need to take down all these layers to understand how my past has informed my present.

Up north, not getting married in a church meant that you were either poor, or divorced and remarrying. In many people's eyes, both were shameful positions to be in. Not that the eyes of those many people had the right to decide what was shameful or not – I often think I saw some of the most unchristian behaviours inside those hallowed Christian institutions. I don't mean fucking in the school chapel (that's legendary) – I mean some of the aspersions cast, and the reasons for their casting, seemed completely outrageous to me as young Christian. Like when my old Sunday school teacher found out I was gay, she told my mum she thought it was 'such a great loss'. When my grandma's devout friend Bill heard she was housing a young woman who had run away from an abusive home life, he told her that 'perhaps she deserved it'. When a friend from church's mother decided to get divorced from her first husband, her father (a Methodist minister and a doctor) told her he'd rather prescribe her anti-depressants for the rest of her life than see her divorced. Growing up, I saw lots of harmful cultures perpetuated by people in the name of religion. But it always baffled me that these harmful cultures contradicted the teachings of the religion itself.

This is where religion is a problem. It's such an obvious thing to say, but it's when the mechanism of control and organisation becomes so great that it ends up chastising any person who has sought a different mechanism of control and organisation. We see people being murdered in the name of it, we see others cast out of communities because of it, we see extremist religious groups picketing gay people's funerals to remind their families that hell is what awaits them.

I've been fascinated by this practice for a long time: by the unchristian Christians I grew up around. The ones who are desperate for the church to thrive, and yet seem to be intent on driving people who disagree with them away. During the course of writing this chapter, I tried for weeks to get in touch with the priest from my childhood church – but, on further investigation, it turned out he had died.

So instead I decided to seek out the world's most homophobic church. The Westboro Baptist Church. Or, perhaps better known as godhatesfags.com. A domain name I find hilarious, one that could just as easily be a website for a Christian fundamentalist group as it could be a religious role-play gay porn site. I first became aware of the WBC some five or so years ago when I watched a Louis Theroux documentary on them. They're that heady mix of terrifying and laughable, and I'd find myself hovering over the send button of their 'media enquiries' email address for a good three days before I took the plunge and did it.

It would be easy to write the Westboro Baptist Church off as delusional extremists, but they kind of do it to themselves. And, really, I spent a lot of time debating whether or not to include this interview here – questioning whether theirs is an irresponsible representation of Christianity. But as a group so publicly committed to the notion of marriage as sacrosanct, I find their obsession with it somewhat revealing. Methinks the ladies doth protest a little too much. And so I decided to do with them what they do with me: to use them as a symbol of just how subjective reality can be.

First of all, I needed them to lay out their definition of marriage, backed by their literal interpretation of the Bible.

'Established in the Garden of Eden by God,' says a representative of the church who goes by the moniker Ezekiel 2:3–8 (a chapter I don't dare look up), '[marriage] is this: One Man; One Woman; For Life. See the Bible, for example at Genesis 2:22 "And the rib, which the LORD God had taken from man, made he a woman, and brought her unto the man. 23 And Adam said, This is now bone of my bones, and flesh of my flesh: she shall be called Woman, because she was taken out of Man. 24 Therefore shall a man leave his father and his mother, and shall cleave unto his wife: and they shall be one flesh."'

It's all rather intense to be honest. But also, it's not necessarily true – and in fact a close reading of the history of marriage tells us that there wasn't really a religious ceremony until the 8th century, and the sacramental nature of marriage wasn't technically written into Canon Law until way later – in 1563, at the Council of Trent, where Catholic dudes would meet to write up laws. Given that Adam and Eve lived, if they ever really did live, between 9,700 years ago and 156,000 years ago depending on who you ask, it's quite hard to trace marriage back to that apple-loving icon and that ribless hunk. And while Genesis 2:22 tells us about the creation of Eve; there is no marriage ceremony described, either implicitly or explicitly. Adam and Eve become man and wife, rather, by default: because he was the only man and she was the only woman.

I don't judge the Westboro Baptist Church, and my new mate Ezekiel, for believing marriage to be natural: that's just subjective worldview. It's impossible for one person to judge another's fundamental ontological belief systems because then you get into the messy and largely racist and homophobic minefield of pitting different subjectivities as having more value, or moral good, than other subjectivities. But what you can judge, with absolute gay abandon, is the ways other people's fundamental beliefs are weaponised to create harm.

Why is this different? What if someone's fundamental, subjective world view is to harm someone else? Well it's kind of open season then, because one subjective worldview therein takes precedent over another's and that, by process of simple deduction, means that respect for subjectivities becomes somewhat null and void.

I clench my fists, looking at the next question I've pre-written. Do I dare? Fuck it. 'What are the WBC's views on gay marriage? Do you think its now-wide cultural and legal acceptance compromises the sanctity of marriage between a man and a woman?' I don't even dare open my eyes.

'We have literally spent decades answering this question on the web page, in sermons, and daily street preaching. I refer you to that. In the simplest terms see the first answer above.

'In short it is abomination and will inevitably lead to the destruction of every society that adopts it, as clearly manifested in the threatenings and examples of the Bible. The antediluvian [pre the flood!] world and the men of Sodom engaged in such practice, resulting in their universal destruction. Jesus Christ reminds us of this reality and eternal truth of God at Matthew 24 and Luke 17. The prophets and apostles regularly remind us of this eternal truth, also. Sodomite marriage is feeble man's attempt at a smash-mouth insult to God.'

Smash-mouth. I'll be using that. The truth is that their rhetoric is incredibly dangerous, although the sting is often removed because very few people take this bunch of white men seriously, myself included. And while indeed the Bible does, in some random line somewhere in the Old Testament, say that men shouldn't bang, it's easy to leave this command behind the moment you think: what does the Bible say about respecting the dead? Quite a lot. And Ezekiel 2: 3–8, when he's leading a protest at a funeral, is, one could say, attempting a smash-mouth insult to God.

Their commitment to marriage is something I find telling about the heart of the institution, though.

So many of us are complicit (myself included) in upholding the belief that marriage is natural, that it is pre-destined, when really it is the only ritual which is completely constructed by man. Birth is real, death is real, even love is (kinda) real: but marriage is a mechanism of social order – something created to build nations, and to form hierarchies of power: whether religious or social. Therein, much like the Westboro Baptist Church, marriage is inherently right wing. A structure made, and upheld, by most institutions be they religious, legal, social and even educational. A quick call to my friend who teaches a reception class, and she tells me that yes – in the very first term of primary school she is required to give lessons on marriage. A site of contention too, because when she gives it she includes gay marriage: something that a lot of the parents weren't too happy about.

But much like the WBC, why is the world so frightened of criticising marriage? Because they believe that if it's unpicked, society as we know it will fall apart.

When I try to question Eze, my new girlie, about the inequalities that marriage creates – explaining that surely God wouldn't want such suffering laid bare on so many of his children – they can't handle the criticism.

'The question is jibber-jabber,' another phrase I should use more often, likely when someone questions me about my gender. 'Worse, it is blasphemous. If you read the Bible, you know that marriage is perfectly established and glorious in every aspect and administration of it. A completely depraved, debauched and morally bankrupt society of people frame up such blasphemous questions, like Judah in the time before their destruction by the hands of the Babylonians.'

Methinks the lady doth protest too much, again.

Until the middle of the 1700s in England, marriages could take place anywhere provided they were conducted in front of an ordained clergyman of the Church of England. But this posed a problem to the state, allowing many marriages to happen in secret – marriages which didn't need parental consent, other marriages which turned out (as there was no centralised record) to be bigamous. This meant couples could marry while one partner was underage, and, when done in secret, it meant that whole family fortunes were lost on the backs of heirs who had fallen in love a little too young, and with someone a little too gold-digging. Love likes to see redistribution of wealth, the state doesn't.

And so in 1753, it became law under the Marriage Act that all marriage ceremonies must be conducted by a minister in a parish or chapel of the Church of England in order to be legally binding. And so, church and state were unified in their want to control how assets were divided, which class could marry which, and how they could maintain a well-ordered society. And while Jews and Quakers were exempt from this law – and their marriages in their respective places of worship were legally binding – Catholics and Roman Catholics had to be married in Anglican churches.

By the 1800s there was much dissent from the Christian faith, with people leaving religion altogether, and so in order to face up to the very real threat non-believers or religious non-conformists posed to the entire institution, Parliament legalised non-religious civil marriages to be held in registry offices across the country.

We can literally see the state learning that in order to keep on top of its people it had to adapt; it was more important to keep people opting in to marriage, as it was such an essential part of state control. Again, in 1929, after a large campaign by the National Union of Societies for Equal Citizenship, Parliament raised the age limit to sixteen for those looking to get married, arguably the only protective measure afforded marrying folk thus far in its recorded history.

Then, other than the gigantic cultural shifts that occurred between 1929 and 2004, nothing about marriage law changed in the UK. Until the gays gained visibility and the world went from ignoring the AIDS crisis in the '80s, to churning out witty gay wedding cards in barely thirty years. A lot of queer people with faith found ways to fuse both identities and get married in a religious context which flowed fluidly around them. But whether religious institutions married us or not, it didn't matter, because the state had widened the net of control, and had welcomed our unnaturalness into its natural, wedded bosom.

It's clear that marriage is a creation. One which we have culturally constructed to offer purpose.

So the question I am faced with is what is natural? And what is natural to each person is different. The more time I've spent in the queer community, the more I've leaned towards the idea that the very concept of 'natural' doesn't exist. That 'natural' is used as a way to disprove homosexuality in pale, stale, male debates about nature and nurture. It's used to refute the existence of trans people, in pointless conversations about biology over far more important things like healthcare, and safety. But natural doesn't exist: our bodies are now made up of hearing aids, hormones, pacemakers; we hold iPhones and use electricity to power cars, doors, even aid plant growth. We eat processed meat and we drink coffees which come out of tiny little metal pods. We flat-pack weddings and fly thousands of miles on honeymoons. Nothing is natural. And why should it be?

Except perhaps our experiences. And one of the experiences I have ignored in my life is that of a religious upbringing. Much like so many of us have ignored how interlinked our value systems are with religion. For such a long time, queerness and my exploration of it took centre stage – and my religion, even the cultural bit – was pushed behind the curtain. But the experience of growing up Christian is natural to me: it has weaved itself around my experiences, for two-thirds of my life, and has an effect on my choices. Some of these things can be questioned, stopped in their tracks, but other – the more subliminal ones – are pretty hard to excoriate from the psyche, especially when you don't realise they're there.

This is why I am so fascinated by marriage. Why I feel such an inexplicable pull towards it, despite the fact that I know it is a system of control. And that pull could easily be mistaken as something natural to me, which is why so many of us who haven't been pulled towards more marginal systems and experiences – like, say, queerness – rarely ask the questions we must be asking about marriage.

And despite all my questioning, my consciousness of the failings of the institution and all the dreadful ways it limits us, there's an inherent emotional want. But is wanting something enough of a reason to do it? In upending the reasons for this want: the way the Holy Trinity of culture, education and emotion compound into one seductive place, I wonder if a want can ever be changed or denied. Experience teaches us that we can learn to want different things, but what if we don't want to stop wanting them? What if there's a part of me that needs to admit that what I want is actually marriage, and this obsession with asking questions of it is just a means to help me find a stand-up reason to justify that want? I'm confused, conflicted. And I can't quite get close to an answer.

But maybe that's the point of this entire exercise. Zach's story demonstrates the power of questioning. Seeing marriage not as definite, but as a vehicle via which to ask questions. Perhaps getting married isn't the part we should be focusing on. But instead, once inside the institution, we have to keep asking questions until we find an answer. So rather than being obsessed with eternity and forever (something religion and marriage have in common), maybe a valuable approach is much more fluid.

So what if the outcome is wrong? So what if we find answers we didn't think we would find? So what if we realise marriage isn't all it's cracked up to be?

Well, that's fine then. Because you can always get a divorce ...

8

Forever, Over

DIVORCE IS MY FAVOURITE part of marriage. Perhaps it's because it's culturally pre-determined that I, a homosexual, love the problematic tabloid stories of messy celebrity divorces, the idea of losing my rich husband in a mysterious accident, Anna Nicole Smith.

Or perhaps it's because divorced people exist in a very specific liminal space – one that is not singledom, nor partnership. To describe someone as a divorcé(e) is, first of all, incredibly chic – especially if they've had more than two divorces – but it's also the only way to be single and not be described using a word which is synonymous with 'lacking'. Cruelly, people who aren't partnered are relegated by society to the place of judgement with words such as 'alone', 'looking', 'single', 'unpartnered' – framing the practice of singledom as analogous to unhappiness. And while divorce befalls certain other stereotypes, at least it's one of the only relationship statuses that allows you to wear a marabou robe, buy a chaise lounge and drink in the morning.

But really, divorce, while not being partnered, speaks to having done the looking, having not been alone, having found fulfilment in the typical way society tells us we'll find it and then making a choice which shows those around you that fulfilment did not lie where we had been told it would. Naturally not all divorces are like this – not every one is a Joan Collins exclusive interview with *Hello!*, or Katie Price writing another autobiography about another marriage gone to the dogs. But there's something enthralling about divorce – something which speaks to choice and power, in the way that marriage certainly does not.

The cultural imagination of the divorcée, in the gay world at least, is one reserved for women. Of course there's a complex vine of misogyny which wraps itself around this particular gay narrative, but since gay divorce hasn't really entered the cultural imagination yet we have to work with what we've got.

And so I've always imagined divorce with a kind of lightness. Much like I imagined myself to be a blushing bride, I imagined myself to be a brutal and botoxed divorcée. Ace and I differ. His fear of marriage comes from the fact that if you do it you do it. 'Committing to forever is huge,' he says in the kitchen as we heat a tin of Heinz tomato soup (you can't beat it), 'not that I'm not committed to you forever, but to get married is to really do that. And once you've done that you can't really go back on the promise.' I find this bizarre coming from someone who has claimed this whole time not to believe in marriage.

'So you don't believe in marriage, but if you do get married you believe in forever?' Clearly Ace hasn't thought about this as much as I have. And perhaps it's because I've always had a penchant for a Jackie Collins novel, or it's because my mum's marriage to my dad was her second – and successful – marriage that I can understand that there is life after (the) death (of a marriage). But the purpose of marriage to me seems less and less about being together forever, it's more a commitment to try to be together forever. And if it fails – much like my career as a maître d' at a wanky London art-space-cum-cafe – then it fails. Then you imagine something else.

Perhaps this is because I have existed on more of a spectrum of failure than Ace. Not that he hasn't failed – indeed I filmed the self-tape he did for a Danish cop show, and it was, suffice to say, a failure – but I've been fat, spotty, poor and trans and thus a failure in society's eyes. He's devilishly handsome and comfortably middle class and his parents welcomed his homosexuality with open arms.

I am interested in our imagination when it comes to marriage and divorce: how we imagine our future(s) after one ends. Who are we when our belief systems – like Ace's belief that marriage has to be forever – are dissolved along with your marriage?

'My divorce was worse than when my mother died.' Meet Linda. She's fifty-one, and her divorce was finalised six years ago. 'I'm still reeling from the whole thing even though it was all initiated by me.'

Linda was happily married for twenty-two years, to a man who was as loving as he was generous: very. She describes her life, at least the early married years – 'the first nineteen' – as 'idyllic'. She's not comfortable saying more than that about the happy times, but the implication is that it worked – the whole smug-marrieds thing – for a decade and a half. And then everything changed.

'He was older than me, only by seven years, but after we hit middle age things started to change. He was itchy,' – from her intonation I think Linda means that he was an arsehole – 'and I was desperate to stop his itching. I became jealous and controlling, and he became distant and patronising. Up until then we'd been intellectually well matched, and while I had stayed at home to raise a child and tried my hand at amateur dramatics, he had always been so grateful for that and had been aware that we both worked – me as a mum, him as the owner of a construction company – and that our work was equally important.'

But then Linda's daughter went to university, and something in their marriage changed. 'He began to see me as purposeless, and I began to see him as ungrateful.' They tried to make it work for two years, and then they tried no more.

Linda fits into a different cultural stereotype: the divorced woman who lost everything. Of course she is much more than that, but the way she thinks of this divorce is very much through a lens of loss.

'The divorce was ugly,' Linda recalls, evidently still badly bruised from how the largest portion of her life had ended. 'He said things to me in that process that I thought he would never think – things about my worth and my work and the time I'd spent raising our daughter while he worked.'

Linda's divorce isn't a special one. It wasn't big bucks or public press chases. It saw her life as she'd expected it razed to the ground, and everything she'd believed since she was a child was put through a 'meat mincer', to use her words. 'I had believed in marriage, and when I promised forever, I promised forever. Another option had never really been presented to me.'

Now Linda is dating, but she's not really enjoying it. 'I lost friends, I lost extended family, I lost a life I'd built with such love and care – and hope, right? It was all gone. Yes I'm less unhappy than I was for those final years, and this is right, where I am now is right, but it's impossible not to feel like I exist on an axis of loss now. Like so much I once loved is lost. Like I've lost more than I have now. Does that make sense?'

It does make sense, when you consider that – according to the Holmes-Rahe stress scale, developed by the American Institute of Stress – divorce is the most stressful thing that can happen to a person, second only to the death of a spouse. Of course, it seems frivolous to compare the two, but divorce – in the case of people like Linda and most people who don't live within a framework where divorce is as expected as the next marriage – is certainly a kind of bereavement. Not only a bereavement for a lost relationship, but a bereavement for your beliefs, for your hope, for your worldview. At least with death you aren't losing your structural beliefs. You made it to forever, pretty much. With divorce you didn't.

If you are someone who had faith in the structure of marriage and then it falls apart, at say forty-five, like it did for Linda, it must be like losing your religion. 'It was. And without it I'm not sure who I am anymore.'

Of course I tell Linda she's many things, but she's heard them all before. I try the old 'you don't need a man' tact, and she responds, 'even if I did, no man will take me darling'. While divorce is a process of empowerment for many women and men, it's also a process of complete decimation for others.

Portia had a different experience to Linda. 'I thought a piece of paper would make no difference. But oh my god, did that piece of paper make a difference!'

Portia is the mother of one of my friends. She'd been married to the same man – the formidable father of my friend – since her late twenties. They'd been happy, if perhaps a little obsessed with the idea of perfection. From the outside it seemed like they had achieved just that: they had the perfect home, the best kids ever, he was fascinating and deeply alluring and she was funny, charming and intellectually engaged. They had the most beautiful home, and the most beautiful life. Then one normal night there was a knock at the door – it was the police – and everything changed.

But that's not what we're here to talk about. We're here to talk about Portia's divorce. Something, she says, she never imagined would have been even a possibility in her mind. Her mother was happily married, her grandmother was happily married, plus she was raised Spanish Catholic, and all of the women around her had presented a life of both ease and easy perfection.

'When the paper came though I felt reborn, I no longer felt guilt for being divorced. I felt that this was my opportunity to start anew and I even remember, the night after my divorce came through, sleeping so soundly. And I woke up feeling so much better than I had before.'

It's not that she resented her husband, and it's not that what happened between them was unforgivable, it's just that Portia decided to stop being good. 'I suppose in my own particular circumstances I wanted to be good. I don't know why. But I wanted to be good. I wanted to be a good mother. I wanted to be a good wife. And I also wanted to be good at my job. But after everything I had a moment to stop and assess the fact that I'd changed. And something I realised: I no longer cared about being good.'

Perhaps what Portia is describing here is the fundamental misunderstanding of marriage. Not a good or bad balance – we're all a bit of both. But the fact that the balances that we establish at the earliest parts of our relationships naturally re-equilibrate over time. For Portia she wanted to be good – a good wife, a good mother, a good woman with an expected place in society – and then she didn't.

One of the fundamental problems with the way we imagine marriage is that we see it as a solidification: a commitment in a relationship that says, 'I'm marrying this person, and my life will be with this person forever.' What that ideology gives no room for is the ebb and flow of either individual or the couple over time. The only constant in a person, and a personality, is change – so often when change comes knocking, or it aggregates over time, we wake up and realise we are no longer wedded to the person we said our I dos to, no longer the same person who said those I dos and no longer want the same things.

This fundamental change – whether vast or minute – which occurs in us all is one of the main reasons most marriages (42 per cent in the UK and 39 per cent in the USA) – end in divorce. Because we wake up one day and both parties have seemingly broken promises. But the promise was never not to change, that's just how we've imagined it.

Not that I'm trying to keep unhappy couples married but I can't help but imagine that if one of the central tenets of marriage and the ways we perceive the idea of forever was that it existed on an axis of change, rather than an axis of security and solidity, maybe we would be less shocked when things actually do ... change. Perhaps we would encourage our partners to seek out change, to lean into it, to understand it. Or perhaps we would accept the change and accept the fact that a divorce is necessary, rather than something to be deemed as a failing. Maybe divorce, in fact, is the ultimate success – strength and humility enough to choose happiness over stagnation, freedom over convention, yourself over something which stopped being good for you some time ago, yourself over the impossible idea of being, to quote Portia, 'good'.

'The thing is that you have a script, and when you marry you're following the script,' Portia continues. 'And even though I didn't think of myself as a person who follows a script, for whatever reason, you realise after being married for a while that you're following a script. And somehow, at some point, you become this team and you kind of buy into the team, and don't want to let the side down. I'm pretty honest with my friends, but it's really only been much later in life, and actually only when people started getting divorced, that we would discuss things about our marriages. It's almost like it becomes too hard to then be honest about it when you're married. You don't want to unpick it. And I think that's something to do with the institution of marriage. I don't think that happens in the same way if you're just with someone and not married.'

Portia found marriage at a time in her life when it allowed her to make the smooth transition from adulthood into proper adulthood: she was a career person in Los Angeles, and she wanted to have children yet forge on with her work in law. So she got married – because she loved her husband-to-be, but it also allowed her to get a visa. But then, over time, things slide: 'there was this sense that his career mattered more, or his potential mattered more. And so I raised the children, did the organising, and he worked. He never asked me to, it just happened.'

While we see marriage as romantic, a thing we do to show our commitment to each other in a tangible way, it's also a kind of smoothing mechanism: ushering people into the next phases of life with ease – allowing us to have children and cohabit with fewer questions asked. But just like we are smoothed into marriage, we are smoothed into normality, reproduction and, in many cases, inequality. We are not only smoothed into them socially, but also psychologically – and these dynamics that so many people find themselves reporting after the end of a marriage, ones where one person takes priority and another takes on all the care, for example – happen smoothly too. There's no day where we wake up and realise our life has changed, or realise what we've compromised or given up for someone, it is – as Portia says – with hindsight only that we are allowed to process the things these institutions have taken from us, and the psychological shifts they have created within us.

This is a huge fear when it comes to marriage. Sure, you can promise each other that you will never become one of those couples – all inequity, silent labour, unspoken resentments – but how can you ever know? You can promise yourself and your future to someone, but how can you know what that future looks like, and if you'll be able to make room for the changes both of you undergo? Because otherwise, you're fifty and you've spent too long hating someone you once loved enough to give your future to. To me that feels like such a painful waste of life.

For Portia, she slid smoothly into this post-reproduction lifestyle without asking too many questions, simply because there wasn't enough time to ask them. And now she's here, with the gift of hindsight, a piece of paper confirming her divorce, and a choice to live her life for her. 'Listen, resentments kind of build over time. Do I wish I hadn't got divorced? No, actually, I think I have an opportunity to take my life in my own direction going forward. But it is sad. That my marriage went the way it went, I suppose. And I suppose I take some responsibility as well for that, because perhaps I was very angry for a while because I hadn't completely fulfilled what I wanted to do.'

Now, having always wanted to be a writer, she's written a book and has got an agent. She's more fun at parties, she dates, she tells raucous stories about the five different types of Steves (read: middle-aged heterosexual men) that she's dating. Her life is a rejection of the stereotypes we associate with divorced women in their late fifties. 'I think there's a sort of fall from grace in the eyes of those around you, and you can choose to see it that way, or you can choose to absolutely ignore it. But I know, I know for a fact, that as a divorced woman of my age, even though I couldn't give two fucks about it, a lot of times you don't get invited to things in the same way that you would as a couple. There are a lot of people who, it's not that they don't want to be your friend, it's almost that they're frightened you're gonna go off with their husband. Or that your presence as a happy divorcée invites questions into their marriage that they're not willing to look at.'

It's evident Portia derives a sort of power from this role as the divorced and newly fabulous woman, a role she admits to playing with alacrity. Of course Portia has what a lot of divorced women don't have – and that's money, something she's grateful for.

Once again the cultural vision of the woman who wins at divorce goes hand in hand with a woman who is very wealthy, because she got an attorney who's a shark and so won more than half of her ex-husband's company. But really this system of divorce, which paints it out to be more like a war between two once-allied countries and a contest to see who can get the most, fails so many who aren't perhaps wealthy enough to become the ball-busting divorcée. Portia's divorce was fairly amicable and she was taken care of financially. For many of those higher up on the economic ladder, divorce can be simple because there's enough cash to go around.

And this is where divorce does its job. And indeed it does have a job; much like marriage does, when it works. That job is protection. If marriage says we will provide for each other, shelter and shield each other, divorce says thank you for that, and it appreciates that that protection cannot be taken away just because a relationship is over.

'Since the millennium, two cases have structurally changed English divorce law from being largely a low-rent sector with smallish, needs-based payouts completely determined by judges in their absolute discretion, and made it the biggest financial event in most people's lives.'

Ayesha Vardag is Britain's top divorce lawyer. She rose to fame for winning the landmark Supreme Court case of Radmacher v Granatino in 2010, and she is the founder and president of the firm Vardags. Over email she tells me the story of these changing protections.

'Upon the millennium, a seismic shift changed divorce law in England fundamentally. The case of White v White injected the principle of equality into the law – there is to be no discrimination between breadwinner and homemaker, and assets built up during the marriage are broadly to be shared equally – the 50-50 split. A decade later, the Supreme Court made another quantum leap, and my case of Radmacher v Granatino established the principle of autonomy in divorce law – couples are free to agree their own marriage contracts (prenups and post-nups), and those contracts are binding unless unfair.'

And so divorce became a safer space for those who had, like Portia, done the work but hadn't been paid for it.

'From White v White onwards, divorce became potentially the equivalent of a 50 per cent tax on all the richer parties' net assets built up during the marriage. The super-rich who had flocked to London, bringing their investment and their consumer spending, attracted by the favourable non-dom tax regime, found themselves asset-stripped when their spouses took advantage of the 50-50 sharing principle and divorced in England. Across the country there was a new cadre of wives, and statistically it was still predominantly wives, though there were exceptions, getting rich beyond their wildest dreams on half the marital wealth. In some cases those wives had worked shoulder to shoulder with their husbands, albeit sometimes in different roles, in others the wives might be said to have contributed very little, the children brought up by nannies, spending their days lunching and shopping and ultimately going off with the tennis coach – those wives were entitled to their 50-50 share effectively for just being married over the period. This is still the current state of the law.'

Of course, where money's at risk, rich people cotton on – and Vardag began to see a change in marriage patterns. 'Naturally this made richer parties reluctant to marry. The 1960s and '70s took the stigma out of unmarried sex and cohabitation, and the 1980s and '90s removed the stigma from having children outside marriage. So there we were, in the new millennium, with no social pressure to marry, and people were opting not to, to avoid giving a giant blank cheque to their partners for the court to fill out as it saw fit. Of course, the result of that was that the financially weaker parties were left without the legal protection of marriage and could find themselves dumped after a twenty-year cohabiting relationship to a multi-millionaire, having brought up many children, and end up on the streets.'

So Vardag took on the fight to make it less financially risky for certain parties to marry by fighting for the consideration of pre and post-nups to be recognised in England, the way they were basically everywhere else.

'The Radmacher case, in which I acted for German heiress Katrin Radmacher who sought to enforce her prenup to protect her alleged £100 million fortune, came at the right time, I believe. Although the law was against prenups as contrary to public policy (because they contemplated divorce) and supposedly disadvantageous to women, there was, I felt, a shift in the zeitgeist, and a sense that something ought to be done to enable marriage without it carrying an implication of financial ruin and to bring England into line with the rest of the world where prenups are commonplace to varying degrees. My own view, accepted by the Court of Appeal, was that to see prenups as disadvantageous to women was paternalistic and patronising, and if women rightly expect equal power and opportunity in the world they have to accept responsibility for their own decisions too; the courts should not assume they are so desperate to marry that they will agree to anything and shouldn't be held to their bargains. I pushed on all these points and it transpired that the door was open. The courts accepted Katrin Radmacher's prenup and this began a new era of autonomy in marriage. Prenups are now part of sensible wealth planning, like wills and life insurance, and couples are free to agree between them a way to marry without risking the acrimony and uncertainty of divorce by agreeing between them in the best of times what will happen in the worst of times. Thus we still have giant 50-50 payouts, transforming the wealth profiles of the country with massive redistributions, sometimes so large and complicated they seem more like global corporate demergers than domestic partings. But for couples with foresight there is the alternative of agreeing to marry on the basis of a contract they both accept as fair.'

But what about the women who don't have money? What about the people who are neither protected in marriage, nor in divorce? Or what about the people for whom divorce is nigh on impossible: because of economics, religion, social stigma? There are fewer stereotypes about the divorced woman who is forced to cohabit with a partner, or the divorced woman who has fallen into poverty because of legal fees and a man who refuses to pay alimony.

This was what happened to my best friend's mum from Lancaster. She and her first husband – the father of two of her children – divorced after a short marriage. It wasn't so good for a while, and so she left him even though he didn't pay her a penny of child support or alimony, and her father told her he would never speak to her again if she signed on the dotted line. So she ended up in a one-bed flat with two young children, a full-time job, and countless favours asked from those close to her to provide childcare. She was pushed to the breadline, and while she was young enough to move away from that line eventually, neither marriage nor divorce provided her with the protections they promised. In fact, it left her worse off.

Despite the culturally mis-held idea that women make it out of divorce better off than men, in actual fact women who worked before or during their marriage statistically see a 20 per cent decline in income according to a paper published by the London School of Economics in 2015. Men, on the other hand, see their incomes rise more than 30 per cent after a divorce. And the poverty rate post-divorce is 27 per cent for women – triple that of men.

The average cost of a divorce is somewhere between £15,000 and £40,000 – and the difficulties of that cost most frequently fall to women because, more often than not, the women in a marriage that is ending have likely given up their job – much like Portia and Linda – and have no access to funds. This is the same for countless working-class women who make more money from child support and caring for their children their selves, than if they were to work full time and pay for childcare. In the UK the average family spends 27 per cent of their income on childcare, in comparison to 13 per cent in Europe. So you forego a job, you claim benefits, and you take care of the kids. And when a divorce is needed you simply can't afford it. I have, and bear in mind I'm twenty-nine, three friends for whom this is the case. All separated, none divorced, all in absolutely loathsome scenarios with their exes.

In America – where, like most things, divorce is an industrial-scale business – there's companies that now offer divorce loans to women. Loans which will pay legal and admin fees because these women have been cut off from access to money. Of course many of the loans companies sell are based on the idea that their clients often receive triple what they're lent in a settlement, but for those for whom that is not a reality, they end up both with less money and mounting debt.

And then of course there are those who are simply too poor to divorce altogether. In the UK, this isn't just those living around the breadline, but for so many middle-income families the cost of separation is one thing, but the cost of life after that separation – two houses, two sets of living expenses, and children – is too high to fathom, according to UK-based charity Relate. The same is true in America, with – according to the American Sociological Association – 15 per cent of divorcing people unable to obtain a divorce due to costs. There are countless testimonials online that give tips for surviving a live-in separation, and there are thousands of people still married even after ten years or more of separation. It seems bizarre that eventually a contract wouldn't simply expire when both people want out of it. Just as capitalism monetises marriage, it also monetises exiting it.

And so the state once again fails us: by forcing us into marriage, and then making it embarrassing (at best) and violent (at worst) to get out of it.

So people stay in marriages because of fear: fear of the unknown, fear of social castigation, fear of poverty, and fear of violence. According to a 2014 Gallup poll, women bear the brunt of the negative side effects of divorce. Of 131,159 randomly selected American adults, results found that divorced and separated women had lower levels of wellbeing and higher stress levels in comparison to their male equivalents. In a 2017 report by the UK's Chartered Insurance Institute (thrilling), research found that divorce poses a more significant financial risk to women, because they are more often left 'vulnerable' by decisions made while they were partnered: meaning who works, who earns money, and who doesn't. The average divorced woman has less than a third of the pension wealth of the average divorced man, and will rely solely on state pensions while a further 41 per cent of men will have an occupational pension to boot. Add social stigmas and increased care responsibilities, plus the common loss of – or need to sell – the family home, and the hostility in the job market towards women over a certain age, and divorce can be a very serious factor for women on an economic level. And while these feel like severely dull realities when written down, these are the kinds of things nobody thinks about while planning their dream day despite the fact that all of this is far more impactful to a life than getting married in the first place. A marriage, it seems, is the biggest economic risk a woman can take.

This is yet another cultural misnomer: with countless incel-lite websites banging on about how divorce always favours the woman. With people arguing that marriage is a financially responsible decision. With us being fed the belief that our relationship is special enough to avoid divorce; that we won't be part of that statistic.

So I come back to the question that seems unanswerable: why are we getting married? And beyond that, if we know why, why are we wearing blindfolds while we do it? To me it seems baffling that there isn't a marriage and divorce course, something which we should be offered by the state to ensure we are aware of the risks we are taking before stepping into a wedding gown. In many religious practices you have to have marriage preparatory courses, but these certainly – if what Holly tells me is true – don't prepare you for divorce. They don't tell the woman to stay at work, to keep her own money aside. They don't tell the man to protect his mental health.

But that will never happen because, much like marriage offers social order, the divorce-industrial complex is a business – one which, of course – benefits the state.

Even in the UK getting a divorce is quite the hefty and harsh task – and until new legislation came in in 2019, the law required one spouse to prove another was responsible for the breakdown of a marriage either by way of adultery, desertion or unreasonable behaviour. This of course creates this competition we've come to know as divorce: one which is about blame and not about the fact that people, simply, change. Indeed if both parties want to throw in the towel, then they can only legally divorce after a two-year separation – but if one person refuses to agree to the divorce, the other faces a five-year wait to dissolve the union officially.

Marriage is tempting, but getting out of it certainly isn't. And while everybody knows that divorce is an option – a highly likely one, in fact – very few people are happy to believe that theirs is going to be the marriage that ends in the dreaded D-word.

Of course, the same state that provides zero actual aftercare once a marriage is dissolved has also set up a system where it happily benefits from divorce too. In order to obtain a divorce on a governmental level, it will cost a base fee of £550 which goes straight to the government. If there were 90,871 divorces in the UK in 2019, that means the government (rounding up a little) made £50 million from divorce in one year alone. That's 10 per cent of the education budget. In the States there are a million divorces a year and if the bridal industry is worth $52 billion, there's no telling what kind of big money rolls through the divorce industry. But, as is everything, it's big business when you imagine the assets, the fees and the tax paid on all of those things.

And while divorcing women are plagued by stereotype, for men there's what? The bachelor? The disappearing act? The one who dodged a bullet? None of these descriptions really have a ring to them, because, of course, men are allowed to get divorced and escape social judgement and shame, where women are, of course, not. And yet again, even in divorce, there's a script.

For David this proved complicated. Because while there's less of a stereotype for a divorced man, there's also much less sympathy and far fewer structures of support. According to a *BMJ* study, a divorced man's likelihood of mortality from suicide doubles after divorce, whereas there's no significant correlation for women. This is a serious statistic, given that suicide is one of the primary killers of men in the western world. And so there is indeed a cultural assumption – which harms both parties – that men do the divorcing, and women are divorced. Yet according to a 2017 Stanford University study women file for divorce in over 70 per cent of cases.

'For me, I have struggled with mental health,' explains David, who I'm speaking to from his flat in Leicester.

Structurally I have very little time for the complaints of men, but talking to David it becomes clear that his divorce cost him an immediate support network, and hit him in unexpected ways. 'I suppose it was the divorce, really. But the big issue was, also, the concerns I have around my relationship with my son. So I've been in therapy.'

David separated from his wife three years ago, although because neither party was 'to blame' the divorce was only finalised this year. 'When it came through we both said, "actually, this is the best thing we've ever done." You know, having kind of reflected on myself throughout my marriage, I was consistently saying to myself, "I don't want to separate, I'm not happy, but I don't want to end this marriage, because my son needs a family structure to grow up in."'

So David had stayed married for much longer than he should have. In fact, he got married when, really, he shouldn't have. 'We weren't happy even before we got married. I felt like marriage was a way of fixing the relationship. Same with having children: we did it because that's the thing you do. It's the script.'

I wonder how many couples do this. How many couples feel the threads of their relationships unravelling and so use marriage as a means to pull them tight once again. And now David is stuck without a script, and an overwhelming feeling of both guilt and justification that he has torn his family apart, that he has 'selfishly' chosen his happiness over a typical family structure for his son.

It's probably that ingrained social expectation in some ways. 'My parents separated when I was young and I don't really remember living with my dad. And I grew up getting the sense from the culture that that was wrong. He had failed. And then when the same thing happened to me, and it was both that cultural pressure – telling me that I failed – and also that personal measurement, I had so much guilt. It's the right-wing Christian ideal about having a mother and father. And I just feel like that's not based in reality. You're measuring yourself against a fiction. And that's what I was doing for a big part of my marriage. Like I used to say to myself, "I need to stay in this unhappy relationship, because if I don't stay in it for my son, he's going to be unhappy." And so realising that isn't real, that it wasn't based on anything real, was kind of a big moment.'

Today, David would say that the care he and his ex-wife are able to provide for their son is better now they are both happier. A lot of his therapy has been about pulling away from the cultural stereotype of the 'deadbeat dad' – one he says really is prevalent among divorcing men – and realising that in reality things are so much more different than the age-old 'dad left when we were young, and now I have daddy issues' maxim. He's not wrong – and who doesn't have daddy issues? Amirite ladies??

'But it's an easy storytelling device. You know, so much of our culture is learned through media. And so much of media is about telling a satisfying story. And an easy one to put on is a character who comes from a broken home.'

The idea of a broken home is a fallacy: because two-parent households can be just as broken as separated families or disappearing dads. There's no hard-or-fast rule when it comes to what makes a healthy environment for a child to grow up in, or a marriage to thrive in, it's just easier to think there is. It's easier to follow a script.

Perhaps this is an area where not being allowed to be married until five years ago has actually benefited gay and queer people: there's no road map of it going wrong, no cultural stigmas or statistically backed employment inequalities in a post-divorce world. There's no 'deadbeat gay dad' (yet), there's no 'gold-digging gay woman' (yet). And so perhaps slipping through the net because people are too uncomfortable to apply any nuanced thought to the life of a homosexual has worked, for once, in our favour. Of course that's not to say that such structures don't exist; it's likely there will be one higher earner in a gay relationship, for example, or one who does the lion's share of the work at home. But the cultural imagination and economic reality of the divorcée doesn't quite befall us the way it does many heterosexual women, and some men.

Sylvie has been trying to get a divorce for five years. Her ex-wife is currently in the process of taking her to the cleaners – hiding money, doing wild stuff with the house I'm not allowed to mention here for actual legal reasons (the glamour!) and claiming half of Sylvie's recently deceased mum's inheritance. Sylvie rolls her eyes, and calls her ex – unprompted – 'a cunt'.

I ask her if there's anything different about getting gay-divorced compared to getting straight-divorced. 'Nothing, you know, it hasn't felt weird at all being gay and going through it or anything. It feels pretty normalised.'

And while it's kind of funny, really, gay divorce is an equal rights issue just as much as gay marriage is. 'If we've fought for power, and you know, this is all about power, and if you've fought for marriage and civil partnership you have to take everything that comes with it as well. To some extent. And so finance is a kind of power. And I feel a responsibility.'

Divorce is responsibility. If the world has created a set-up where, at its best, marriage offers protection then divorce must mirror that protection. And while single-fault divorces create a contest-like arena, it is the responsibility of the wealthier party to concede that perhaps their wealth was earned on the back of someone else's labour. Sylvie agrees, and is happy to give over half of everything. It's just all the rest that she's pissed off about.

Sylvie was the breadwinner in the relationship – by a large amount. And so now her role in this divorce has become somewhat the typical role of the 'man', or so she says. 'See, honestly, I think what people do is a bit like what they do in gay relationships, they try to assign the typical male and the female roles. So in our case, for instance, I earn a lot of money, my ex doesn't. So I would say I get assigned the typical male role where, you know, he's got the money and she's ... you know ... hoping to get as much as possible out of it. So I think in some ways people just stereotype within gender-specific roles.'

I ask Sylvie if this is frustrating, but she says it's not. 'It's interesting. The most interesting thing is I speak to a lot of women who are in the same position but divorcing their husbands, and they describe their situations and all the hassles they're having, and I keep thinking: well, they're describing me. And I feel like saying "there's two sides!" '

She laughs when she says this, and it's clear that she enjoys being in this position which one might argue, statistically at least, is certainly the more powerful one even though she's being swindled. But here is a gift. Here is where being gay and getting married gives us a one-up over our heterosexual peers: because Sylvie can laugh off the gendered expectation of either the man or the woman because society has excluded us from the cultural idea of the divorcée for so long. This means that while Sylvie's divorce looks the same on paper, her future looks wildly different in real life.

'The future feels different. I mean, we were together twenty years before we split, and we were only married for five. I don't think either of us would say we gave up our life for the other person, we were two individuals that came together and had no children. In fact I think often it's having children that means you end up giving up something. So I certainly didn't. I carried on working. And she'd probably say the same. In terms of the divorce I think I'm just a bit pissed off.'

I ask her why.

'I don't feel like I've wasted the time. I just feel a bit pissed off that I got married in the first place, because I am now set to lose half of my wealth because of it. So whereas I could have retired exceedingly comfortably had we not been married, now I lose half of everything. And for something I wasn't really bothered about either way? God, it's just annoying.'

So why did Sylvie get married? For the same reason a lot of gay people do: to protect themselves in death, to allow for her partner to make decisions about funerals, about hospital visitation and healthcare. 'You get to an age where you think – well, why wouldn't you get married?'

Obviously with hindsight Sylvie wonders if her ex was looking for protections to be cashed in sooner rather than later, whether their marriage was a means of protecting herself in a relationship where the love was evidently dwindling. And, much like most quick-fix last-ditch solutions, it obviously didn't inspire more love.

I'm fascinated by Sylvie's vision of the future. So often, gay people aren't allowed to build that future for themselves. We aren't given a script, and, what's more, we lost a large proportion of a generation to AIDS – and so when we look around there are very few examples of what a gay future looks like. This is something that's both enticing and terrifying.

There's security in not knowing. Or, better put, in knowing that you can't know. It makes you more fluid, more realistic, more committed to living an extraordinary life because there is no script there for us to follow any more. At the same time, it's impossible to imagine growing old. Sure, you can do it on an individual level – predicting wrinkles, and visualising what your face might look like after one too many bad surgeries – but to imagine community, love, partnership when you're old in the way heterosexuals do is hard. And if you can't see it, you can't really be it.

Indeed there's a freedom to it: one which, at the best of times, seems filled with opportunity, with a chance to take your future and make of it what you want: whether that's lifelong promiscuity or monogamy and a rented flat slapped floor to ceiling in Farrow & Ball's premier homosexual colour: Hague Blue. But this freedom can also paradoxically be unmooring: it makes it hard for us to imagine our part in a future where many of our friends will pair off, have children, get divorced. It makes it hard to be sure. While heterosexuals can't be sure of their future, at least they have a pattern. And at least they have cultural stereotypes to fall back on if all else fails. I'm fairly anti-labels but sometimes they sure are helpful.

So how does Sylvie feel about the future?

'Very positive. Really positive. Yeah, I feel like weight has kind of lifted, I guess. You know, in any relationship, whether you're married or not, the last period of time is hideous. And five years of divorcing is not great, either. So as we're getting to the end, I do feel this sense of relief: I love the fact I'm on my own and I love the freedom of

that, and not being responsible for anybody. You don't
realise that perhaps someone controls you to some extent,
they might not mean to, but there's a controlling element
or there's a compromising element. And suddenly, I think,
I don't have to care. I don't have to give a shit about
anybody. You know, I can do whatever I want. I'm not
responsible for anybody. I would say this is probably the
happiest I've been, possibly ever.'

It's thrilling to hear – that Sylvie is free of the weight
of stereotypes, and of her toxic ex. And this extends
to dating – and at this point, I started to well up in our
interview. It's just so infrequent to be presented with a gay
future. I've read about it, I've watched *Grace and Frankie*.
But here was a rare moment where I had proof that what
my community has nurtured for all of these years – radical
love, anti-labels, different manifestations of relationships,
eschewing stereotype and normativity – is as liberating
when you're older as it is for us now. Never mind if it
doesn't fit in the cultural psyche; the script was taken
from us all when we came out and while that's a daunting
thing to get your head around at first, the opportunity to
improvise all the way through life is the kind of liberation
that makes all of the sacrifices that come with an identity
like ours so worth it.

Now Sylvie is dating much more fluidly. 'So we
have this thing. And I think once I said that, this thing
I have with this person is not enough for me, and I did
online dating and then got close to somebody and then
thought: you know what, I want this thing, this non-
relationship I have now. So yeah, I've just sort of muddled
along with this non-relationship, which actually, I decided,
suits me because I don't think I actually want the pressure
of being partnered. You know, most of my friends are

single, or gay. So I'm not in a couple-y world. I'd feel unusual if I were in a partnership, actually, because most of my friends are single.'

'Listen Tom, people talk about a script. But do you want to live that script? I don't want to live that script. And, you know, the most interesting people I know who are older, who are my age, are people who are just out there ... still being interesting.'

I had imagined that marriage forces you to approach normality: to smooth your life down from late nights and orgies and a hectic but fulfilling social life, to nights in with your partner; to holidays with this one; to scrubbing skirting boards and slow psychological shifts where you fantasise about what colour Magimix you're going to order from the catalogue, and not what order you'll be texting your dealer with on a Friday afternoon.

Strangely, divorce gives me hope. Perhaps it's because I'm gay, so – like Sylvie – I can shirk a stereotype, I can refuse to fall into the cultural psyche of divorced and failed, divorced and empowered, divorced and worthy of pity. Instead I can seek fluidity. And can't we all?

Perhaps one of the fundamental issues with marriage is the way it's organised, not the fact that it exists. What if there was a reimagining of it, just for those who want it but aren't sure? What if we protected ourselves financially with separate bank accounts, with a prenup like those Vardag so fiercely championed? And what if this self-protection wasn't a dramatic issue of trust like it's often portrayed in a *Desperate Housewives*-style scenario where one person won't sign a prenup, and another won't marry them unless they do, so they have to prove they are trustworthy by undergoing some serendipitous but perfectly timed test to prove that prenup is a waste of time?

What if self-protection from the ending of a marriage, or the potential of it, was something we cherished in our partners? What if we didn't consider marriage as a merging of assets and lives, as entry into neat and tidy social order, but more as a promise to each other that we would protect where we can and set free where we can?

What if we understood marriage as a bedrock upon which the changing nature of a person could take root and grow, and that growth could be celebrated? What if, when that bedrock could no longer provide the kind of environment needed to allow this change, we saw divorce as another way to protect our partner too? As a way to set someone free, to offer them a chance to continue to change, to show them that there might be more to life than who we were when we said I do?

What if we allowed ourselves to imagine a marriage defined by its scope and not by its limits?

But if the answer was 'sure, let's' then would we even be getting married at all?

9

Audiences

IN THE SUMMER OF (the first) lockdown Ace and I went against our better moral judgement and flew to Corfu for five days. Restrictions had eased, and travel was allowed, and we were in an Air Bridge™ with Greece, so we figured, after deeply anxious deliberation all the way to Heathrow, through check-in, security, the gate, and to our airplane seats – where I said 'we can still get off, do a Rachel?' as the plane began to taxi – that we would go to Corfu in a global pandemic and not tell anyone. We didn't put it on social media, we told only the most trustworthy friends, and we made sure we checked our emails diligently from the beaches in the north-west of the island so as to appear that we were where we'd been for all of lockdown: at home obsessively sanitising the letterbox.

We were far too politically engaged to be travelling. Indeed, confusing messages were sent over social media via some of the most right-on influencers once lockdown had eased: pictures of them nude in a pool in Venice, followed by an infographic about how Summer Has To Stop if we're ever gonna get through this. The truth is, I agreed with the latter. 'But,' we reasoned, 'it's allowed,' staring at each other in severe, mutual disappointment knowing that we'd never trusted the Tory government on anything before, so why were we trusting that they knew it was safe to travel now? And the answer is: because we wanted to.

Because we had discussed every possible and probable outcome. Because we had assumed that, for some self-superior reason, we were exempt from our own moral codes, or the codes that the middle classes so swiftly applied to working-class holidaymakers before jumping on a British Airways flight from Terminal 5 and never looking back. Nothing depicted this more grotesquely than when we arrived at a teeming Terminal 5 and I looked at Ace and said, in genuine disgust, 'can you believe all of these people travelling?' And then we checked our bags.

We'd been very strict over hard lockdown – those first three months my flatmates and I had left the house on a rota once a week for a run or for groceries. We didn't socialise, we disinfected every single lemon, pack of cigarettes, even the bottles of disinfectant that entered the house, and we told friends who wanted to meet us at a distance in local parks that it would absolutely not be possible. As queers, our experiences of the world had primed us for the arrival of the apocalypse, and while things were tough for four working drag performers and a set designer, we adapted swiftly to different ways of life.

We were the lockdown equivalent of a hardcore marriage abolitionist – joyless but correct – and yet, when it eased even slightly, Ace and I were on the plane quicker than a northern bride announces her engagement on Facebook – which my friend from Lancaster Gemma did, during lockdown, a mere five minutes after her husband-to-be had popped the question down on Morecambe prom where we'd done karaoke only a few months ago in a working men's club in front of a home-made sign that read 'Forget We Lest'.

The consequences of our travels were ultimately quite low: we went to Greece, we shuttled between a house and completely dead beach, and we grocery-shopped in masks. We got tested on arrival back to the UK, and we quarantined until we got our results.

And the truth is that the consequences of a marriage between Ace and me, something that's on my mind Now More Than Ever, were very much the same as the consequences of our travel: that nobody, really, cared as much as we did. Nobody, really, is looking. And nothing, really, will change for anyone else if we decide to tie the knot, or travel to Corfu. But once this ideology is extrapolated out and across the population of marrying folk, or to every traveller at Terminal 5, you have a virus which spreads, and hurts a lot of people.

But this is how we make most of our moral decisions, jumping frantically between the individual and the international. One Amazon package is fine, but 197 million (that's how many people buy off Amazon a month, globally) packages creates modern-day slavery and a monstrous billionaire who could solve world hunger but chooses not to. We are at once so aware of the world and what it thinks of us – which is why we keep our pandemic vacays off social media – and yet we are reluctant to grapple with our actual individual effect upon things. One package won't hurt. One person who can't make it to the voting booth won't make a huge amount of difference, but when that mentality is shared by 25 and a quarter million (the number of people who didn't vote in the 2019 election) we end up with a government who thinks herd immunity is what's best for the country in a deadly global pandemic.

I'd spent the best part of two years excavating, self-assessing, being as un-judgementally judgemental about people who got married, and people who didn't, because I'd thought whether one got married or not was an absolute indication of your moral values – are you rock-hard or super-soft? Are you pro the system, or are you against it? Are you clever, like me, and have thought your way out of marriage because it's very very bad, don't you know, or have you been hoodwinked by society into thinking that marriage is the be all and end all? Worse, are you one of those people who was dead against marriage all the way through your twenties because it made you seem more interesting at dinner parties and in club smoking areas and, like clockwork, you get married at thirty because it's what you always wanted, or because you can't take the pressure of being interesting any more.

Someone who has made a career out of this transition – from single to married, with a lot of criticism in between – is writer and creator of *Sex and the City*, Candace Bushnell.

Like most people with a skewed relationship towards love and sex, Candace, her book and the attached TV show played a significant role in my education in love. There was no chance I was getting that at a Catholic state school in Lancaster, where all I remember of sex-ed was a group of visitors coming into an assembly and showing pictures of discoloured todgers while saying 'this is untreated gonorrhoea'. In fairness, I should have listened more because some years later I would find myself admitting my love for Ace on a street in Fitzrovia having just received a text from the GUM clinic confirming that yes, indeed, that burning sensation when you pee is in fact not love, it's 'untreated gonorrhoea'. But *Sex and the City* was my love education, my sex education, and my aspiration education. And no matter how many marriage-abolitionist queers and academics I spoke to, I still tingled with joy when Carrie walked up the steps to her (soon to be ruined) wedding to her Mr Big. Knowing one day this would be me, willing this fantasy into my reality.

I'm sure any therapist would tell me that mapping my own life aspirations onto fictional characters and talented-yet-misunderstood famous women is not how to build a future. But I don't have a therapist so I map away with gay abandon. But this mapping, I would say to my impossibly chic therapist, is something we queers are forced to do. See, the thing about heterosexuals is that they belong to a giant historic structure, and that structure provides them with a script, like Portia said – complete with stage directions – on how to build their future. This isn't to say that having that script doesn't throw up its own set of challenges, especially when you try to rewrite it like Linda or Amanda Teague (ex-Sparrow), but for me there is no dynastic structure or popular envisioning of what it would mean to be old, queer and married. Forever is an impossible concept because I don't know what that looks like. I don't know what old, queer and married looks like. I do, however, know what old, straight and married looks like and that's how you get a Brexit.

245

And yet here I was in the middle of a *Sex and the City* rerun binge, on the cusp of secretly flying to Greece, lying awake long after Ace had fallen asleep wondering where on the island of Corfu I might actually ask him to marry me. To build a forever with me, and write a script with me, and become part of a historic structure with me. I had spent lockdown deeply valuing the sense of security provided to me by my partner: one where all my identity markers faded into the mundanity of the day to day because there were so few encounters where I was made to feel like a failure of a man, a failure of a heterosexual, a failure of a body. And so I'd begun to repurpose the idea of normality and security into something which might be quite radically healing. Maybe, in fact, taking things that aren't meant for you is radical, maybe taking things that are kept from you is revolutionary. Maybe claiming the security, the old age, that I was never promised is an act of defiance against a system that doesn't want me to be safe, secure, protected.

Or perhaps I'm clutching at straws for convenience. Liberatory psychology would tell me that I have to extract the voice of the norm from my head, to rid my head of the system's control and divest from marriage. But the same psychology would, when applied in a different direction, tell me that choosing a future not originally intended for me was a liberatory act in itself.

So I was three days away from my flight, and I was really thinking about doing it. Like really thinking about it: thinking what the hell, thinking why not, thinking that if I did pop the question on a Greek island in secret it would perhaps be less real, thinking that I didn't know if I was ready for this to be real, thinking how many likes a social media announcement would get. I was about to be away from the world, from my own little audience of my flatmates, of my family, of social media, and what I would say to him when I asked him somewhere on a beach late at night kept swirling around my head. Ace none the wiser, asleep next to me and completely unaware of all my thoughts of him. Unaware of all my thoughts about what people would think and say if and when we announced we had got engaged in secret.

I decided I needed to seek advice. I hadn't worked out yet if I really thought this was the right thing for us, for me, for him, for our community and our politic, or whether it was another *Sex and the City*-induced normativity rush. If I was really going to do this, despite all my better judgements and political beliefs, I had to work out if I'd been miseducated by Ms Bradshaw. I had to work out whether those heart clutches and deep-set dreams were the final chokeholds of normality wreaking havoc on my brain chemistry. And so I did what any person with a phone would do and decided to find a therapist. Lol, obviously not! I decided to email Candace Bushnell at 4 a.m. on Tuesday night. No reply. And thank god too, because this is what the email said, spelling errors in bold:

Dear Ms Bushnell,
First, let me state that you are my icon. And not just my icon, but an icon to so **may** girls and gays everywhere. Not only did you teach us about love and sex in an ailing education system, you taught us how to dress, shop, and be completely, unstoppably chic. The episode with Amalita at Balls **Ace*** – inspired.
I am currently in a liminal space – which you might likely be able to pick up on given that I'm emailing your personal address at this hour from the UK. I wish I could

247

say my writing to you was cosmopolitan-induced, but I'm afraid the reason is much less, or perhaps much more, chic depending on the way you look at it.

I'm writing a book about marriage, and I'm on the cusp of proposing to my long-term boyfriend. He's brilliant and wonderful and a far better man than Mr Big (although certainly if Mr Big showed up in Paris during a personal life crisis and after the loss of many of my loose diamonds I too would fall into his arms, although I can't afford Dior).

As previously stated, your book and the legacy of the show, was my education. And I'm on the precipice of reaching the end of Carrie's journey too and I'm asking myself: I do, do I?

I would love to speak to you about this, about marriage, and about your advice on the topic of love and relationships if you'd ever have the time? I'm sure you're **definatly** busy ... but God loves a trier!

Thanks for your time. I hope you are safe and well and drinking a Cosmopolitan somewhere!

Tom xxx

*Turns out my phone autocorrected Balzac to Balls Ace because I had spelled it Ballac. Not chic. But also iconic.

After a deep google the next morning, I found her publicist's email address. And after some persuasion, Bushnell agreed to a call from her home in upstate New York. 'Be forewarned, she's not a fan of weddings,' her publicist advised, and within a day I was on a transatlantic call to one of my (not so) secret heroines, my palms sweating that she was going to tear me apart for even discussing marriage, let alone asking her – as if she were my oracle – whether she thought I should be getting married. Breathe,

Tom, I thought as she picked up the phone – Carrie was never bothered by celebrities, neither are you.

'*Sex and the City* presented a different path for women.' She has the best voice – deeply New York, and impossibly stylish, and as we very seriously discussed this show, her legacy, her stance on marriage I literally kept pinching my arm like bitch this is your gay fantasy you must get her to invite you for a cosmo. But cosmos were the last thing on Bushnell's mind, and we were in a global pandemic. No – we were here to talk about marriage, and her contribution, whether positive or negative, to the culture surrounding it.

'There were a lot of women, certainly in New York City, who had gotten into their thirties and had not found the guy. But interestingly, unlike the characters on *Sex and the City*, most of my friends, like myself, as they moved out of their thirties and into their forties, did end up getting married and having children. *Sex and the City* showed women a different option, than say going to college and then trying to get married in your twenties.'

I don't know if I agree. While *Sex and the City* in many ways did present women with a different option, or perhaps more accurately a different timeline, the end goal of the whole series and the movies was romance, love, partnership and – as evidenced by the fucking ridiculous theatre show that became Carrie's wedding in the first movie – marriage. The aspirations didn't change, perhaps the show even cemented them more immovably in our cultural psyches, but at that time – remember this was the 1990s – perhaps that was enough. And in the end, Carrie was sort of conservatively shamed for wanting all the shiny bits of a wedding that society tells us we must have. 'I let the wedding get bigger than Big.' And so she gets married in a dress by no one, just her and Big. Ugh.

And besides – Bushnell is critical of where the series ended up.

'It was my life until the end of season three. But this is entertainment. You couldn't have an audience following a couple, a love story, for six seasons and have them not end up forever.' Couldn't you? I couldn't help but wonder. And the answer is perhaps, as Candace says, no – because people are seeking an ending which is happy, neat, resolved. Because culture tends towards the normal.

And while a different timeline is a step towards rewriting the script, there are still very few cultural depictions of women and queer people who fully, and happily, chew it up and spit it out altogether. Even a show like *Schitt's Creek* – which I'm obsessed with by the way, you have to watch it, just hang on for the first two episodes – tends towards the normal: yes, the characters' world is wonderful and accepting, but the central gay couple still get married. And so the worrying thing, after a whole new wave of feminism and queer liberation has swept our shores and our politician's T-shirts since *Sex and the City* ended, is that little has changed when it comes to our aspirations. Marriage numbers fall every year, but not by a number significant enough to be worried about. And this isn't really because people aren't getting married – they are just, like Candace's friends, getting married later. And while one might argue that this is directly correlated to a cultural shift created by TV shows like *Sex and the City*, if this is it then culture hasn't shifted too far.

'So we're getting married later, but do you think the content of marriage is actually different?' I ask Candace.

'Look, money is power there's no way around that. And the person who has the money in the relationship is the person who has the power, the person who holds the purse strings. So we have a situation now where women have much more financial independence.' This is interesting, and true across most classes too – even though Candace is certainly talking about high society New York career women who don't quite have the cash to buy their '20-million-dollar houses', but do have the cash to bedeck their walk-in wardrobes with a million in shoes.

'I've always been critical of our culture,' she continues, 'which tells women that marriage and children should be their biggest goal. And, of course, I grew up at a time when that was much more true. I think I said at one point that marriage is a male invention. And it actually was a male invention. I mean, marriage was really about a way for lower-status men to find partners. In terms of nature, women will tend to go for highest height, they're more interested in higher-status males. So in a way, marriage was a way for a male to buy and own a female. That's the core of marriage. And the core of marriage for a woman is a form of prostitution. You do not work, and you supply sex and motherhood and cleaning the house. Right? Really one of the tenets of marriage originally is that you are expected to deliver sex to your husband whenever he wants. You also can be beaten. It was legal to beat your wife, probably up until the sixties or seventies.'

I agree with a lot of what Candace says, but I find it strange that the woman who built an entire kingdom off a character who only obsessed over men (while saying a lot of smart things about the patriarchy while doing it, sure) is so dead against something that forms the backbone of her legacy, or at least an integral vertebra in that backbone.

'Do you think marriage has changed since the time when it was much more of a social contract based on gendered lines than it is now,' I ask. 'Do you not think that inside a marriage there's a different gender structure to how it seems on the outside?'

'Listen, maybe. But once you have kids, then you're in a reproductive lifestyle. And that tends to take over whatever kinds of ideas you may have had about equality. People start off thinking that they're going to have a partner [in a] marriage and a partner [in a] relationship. And what usually happens is that the realities of life get in the way. And when you think: those realities are that the kids have to be dressed and they've gotta go to school, and you've gotta get people places. You've gotta run a household. All of that. People tend to fall back into traditional roles. So I think I've been reading a bit lately on women who find themselves back in traditional roles despite the best intentions. There are just certain realities.'

There are just certain realities. And while many of them don't necessarily create liberatory circumstances for those involved – which is Candace's central issue with the institution of marriage – is liberation what everyone is seeking?

The answer is that liberation looks different to different people. That context, upbringing, education will produce a different understanding of what freedom feels like as per each individual. A major issue with wedding and marriage culture is that we are forced to celebrate it collectively, even if we think it's oppressive.

This is in equal parts perhaps one of the strangest, most harmful and most redeeming parts of the culture. Its celebration. The culture around weddings would have us believe that they have always been huge moments worth celebrating: a kind of graduation into adulthood. Indeed, there was a time before big weddings, but there's now a strange expectation that our love should have an audience.

But believe it or not (and this is a note to myself) there was a time when talking on the internet about the people you'd shagged, and the ways you'd shagged them was not a thing. There was a time before it was socially acceptable to post every move you made with your partner, or share wedding pictures as if they were an emblem of success. Sure, in an arguably revolutionary way, *Sex and the City* allowed those of us not usually permitted to talk about our sex, pleasure, love – namely women, and gays – to do so publicly. So for those of us who grew up on that show we became sharers, we believed our love needed an audience just the way Carrie's had. And we believed there to be political weight in talking about it, just the way Carrie led us to believe. And this is in part true. Public awareness of female pleasure, of queerness and gayness and transness, of different formulations of love, of women who don't want to get married, of sex workers, of women who don't want children, of women who marry themselves, of polyamorous setups and asexuality, has certainly evolved. And just like *Sex and the City* did then, these visibilities set out an alternative pathway for those of us with divergent ideas, desires and needs. But the centre continues to hold, and marriage is very much at the centre of how we conceive of relationships and their trajectories. And while what we're seeing has diversified, support for it hasn't necessarily increased because visibility is a false god.

Visibility has confused my entire twenties. So much so that I have found myself seeking out experiences just for the story of it, so much so that when I was the victim of a homophobic attack and my face was covered in deep red blood and deep red glitter, I spent more time toying with posting an image and a long, emotional caption to Instagram than I did on the actual effects of such an attack. And when I think about big life events, they are skewed by my relationship to how they will appear to an audience. Oftentimes when we do this it's for good cause: we are conscious, and we care. But with something like a proposal for example, I find myself wondering just how many likes an announcement online could garner. Thinking about the perfect caption – something critical, witty, yet full of so much love that even the coldest-hearted anti-marriager would melt like Lurpak into a crumpet. Indeed, we live in an Instagram Panopticon. What would Foucault say?

And it's not just online, we consider the audience in everything we do. When I think about a proposal to Ace, I often find myself imagining what family members and friends would say before I even think about him, and what he would say. Or what he would want.

I realise that my choices have not necessarily been based fully on an internal moral-and-emotional, personal-and-political conflict, but perhaps on how they might be read by those around me who have informed my morals, and those whose morals I have judged. They have been informed by the audience, and not necessarily by myself.

Naturally. For most of my teen years my mantra was 'I don't care what anyone thinks about me' – and I would parade around sharing explicit stories, saying the most outrageous thing possible, while coming hard for my homophobic detractors. When they go low, you go lower. My belief in this mantra certainly saved me through high school, university and the endless examples of street harassment that seemed to follow me throughout my early twenties until I got beaten up badly on my doorstep and decided to dress in camouflage in order to move through space.

But as I grew up, moved into queerer, more political circles and people began to hold me accountable for my behaviours, I became more aware of this audience and what they thought of me. And this real and imagined audience began to alter my behaviour: and in so many good ways. You think 'what would this person feel if I said this' before saying it, and so you're able to be kinder, more respectful, and show up for people who get less thought from society than you. But sometimes that imagined audience becomes too loud and it creates an irrational bar in my mind – like in so many of my generation's minds. And so, like with this marriage question, I was shocked when many people in my imagined audience of marriage naysayers saw things with more nuance than I did. And each of them saw how good Ace and I are together; they saw the benefits of marriage, and thought that in a world of crap there's no more joyful thing than celebrating queer love, and celebrating queer stabilities.

The problem with both of these ways of living – not caring, and caring too much – is that both require an audience, both demand one in order to exist. But what happens when you take the audience away? This seems an unthinkable question, even though so many people I know (a scarily high amount actually) tell me they dream about deleting their Instagram every single day. But we don't, because what if we miss something important, what if it makes us less important?

So nobody could have planned for the removal of this audience – both IRL and URL – when we locked down in March of 2020. Yes, we were all still scrolling our feeds, but our circles got smaller, our ability to fill our life with social engagements and time with others became narrower, and now there was nowhere to go, and no way to tag yourself and your partner at the places you were no longer going. What Ace and I had, which is something that until lockdown millennials had decided was the biggest luxury, the most unattainable aspiration, was time. Time together. What we had was the reality that Candace is talking about, and not the audience that she created.

I live with Ace. And during lockdown – until about a week before we left for Corfu – we had spent every single day and night in our house. We, if my calculations are correct, spent 139 days and nights next to each other. We cooked for each other, cleaned up after each other. We worked next to each other and overheard every work call and family argument had over those 139 days. We hoovered up each other's toenail clippings. We ate every meal together, bar the odd solitary lunch when one of us needed to work through in order to feel busy.

Before lockdown it would often take us three weeks to a month to realise we hadn't spent a single night (bar the sleeping) together. Sure, we might socialise in a group, but to actually do something – just us – we could go thirty-nine days until it hit us we hadn't really asked the other how they were doing. Of course I would talk about our relationship all the time to my friends, and we would go to all the right social events together. Thankfully, I saved myself the public shame of ever actually putting a picture of us smugly photographed outside a World Heritage site anywhere on my social media, but our relationship lived in the real-fake world. We were busy people, and there's nothing I despise more than the creamy feeling you get when a partner forces you to 'stay in bed on a Sunday morning and just … chill'. If anyone's wondering, that's my hell.

But here we were – an unknowable amount of Sunday mornings in bed stretching before us. I'd be lying if I didn't have moments early on where I felt worried at the prospect of spending every waking hour with another person, worried that it might lead to the crashing realisation that you in fact have nothing in common except a love for socialising and not posting on social media and Christine from *Selling Sunset*. But there's only so much time you can spend on Christine before you have to move on to Mary and then that just swiftly becomes about Romain, and that swiftly becomes dull.

And yet the opposite happened.

What does love look like when nobody is looking? I realised, as our social circles were reconfigured and our days spent bitching with friends about how he forgot that you didn't like the chorizo pasta parcels (and like 'does he even know me really guys?'), that I had no idea what we were like, just us two. Of course we spend time together alone, but during lockdown it was almost as if we became a unit – kind of like an intensified marriage where you move to the middle of nowhere and see nobody else.

Naturally, this was bizarre to start with. We live in a time when every corner of my generation is surveyed, where we think about the audience as much as we think about the reality. So much so that the life events that I have written off in this book – marriage, kids, house, the life plan – have become more than simply life events. They have become shareable moments – moments to trumpet online to show that you are living your best life, even though living and online are completely oxymoronic.

But lockdown removed aspiration as we know it, it narrowed our lives drastically and it destroyed all the distractions we put in place in order to make us feel like we were really doing the living. On days when my brain was full of nothing I would switch on the radio, and there you would hear countless callers, day in day out, expressing how they've never felt like this before – some in positive ways, some in negative ways. But the most overriding experience discussed beyond fear of the virus, loss and the shite British government, was people felt like what they wanted, and what they needed, was actually changing for the better. Like they were more focused on meaning, and less distracted by meaningless things like Pret (lol bless Pret it really took a tumble). And is a wedding, at least in its modern formation, not merely another distraction from the realisation that everything that we thought had a point to it is, simply, pointless?

Sariya had this realisation four weeks into lockdown. 'I looked at him and I realised I couldn't do this anymore.' Sariya had married her husband two years ago, and they had never really spent much time together. They had met on Raya – an app for the rich, international elite that doesn't have a location filter because it assumes you can afford to fly anywhere for a date. 'The longest we'd ever been in the same place was two weeks. And even in those two weeks we would have mostly separate plans. And this is what I had wanted: freedom, fun, a good lifestyle and a lovely husband who would fit in with this lifestyle, the way I would fit in with his.'

And my god did they celebrate the union of their lifestyles. Sariya sends me some pictures of her wedding on Instagram while we're on the phone, and I gasp. 'Yes, it seems so silly that we spent so much money on something like this,' and then she sighs – evidently looking at the pictures herself – 'I don't even look happy even though that is a real diamond on my neck.' Once again, I gasp – the diamond she is referring to is perhaps the second-biggest diamond I've seen after the fake heart of the ocean my friend Amnah bought me for my birthday last year.

Sariya had sought a divorce on her couch via text message, while her husband smoked cigars in the next room. 'I just realised I wasn't happy. I was locked in a house with a man who had given me the most picturesque life, and I couldn't share any pictures, and you know, I didn't want to. I couldn't talk to him about it, because – as he confirmed when I told him – he would have been very angry with me but would never have entertained the idea of us trying to make our relationship more meaningful. I had all that I thought I wanted, and it's so funny that when all of the people I used to show that off to could no longer be around, it all became nothing to me. And so did he.'

Sariya is in the process of finalising her divorce, and while her separation was 'complicated', she says she's now feeling much 'clearer' on what it is she really wants. When I ask her what that is, she tells me 'something real'.

And something real is what Florence found during lockdown, very much to her own shock. 'James and me met just before lockdown, in like February, and we had talked very early on about marriage and the future. And then lockdown happened. And we ended up living together in a very, very domestic way. So even though we've been together for about three months, it feels a lot longer than that. Which is weird because it's like we've done it backwards and the domestic part of the relationship that usually comes later has been done now.'

And so they got engaged. After three months. I'd be lying if I didn't say I was judging Florence somewhat for getting engaged so swiftly. But then again, just before we spoke I saw an Instagram story of her wearing a new season studded Prada headband and reasoned therein that she must have good sense because that was the most covetable piece from the SS20 collection. A Prada-buyer is nothing if not intelligent. And so I withheld my judgement, and decided to hear her out.

'I want to marry him because I've had so many shitty relationships with horrible men who treat me so horribly. And James is just the most lovely, kind, sweet man. And I just, I want to be with him for the rest of my life. Does that sound crazy?'

Florence acknowledges the challenges they'll face once lockdown is over: meeting each other's friends, socialising and work, and of course the dreaded jealousy thing. But right now it all appears rather peachy, rather simple. And that's perhaps because nobody else is involved. Because neither of them were thinking of what anyone else would think. Because that audience has been removed.

'We weren't really going to tell anyone about the engagement. Now I feel more open to talking about it because I feel like people will respect that more because we've lived together. But I haven't told a lot of my friends because I think I'm worried about their judgement about the speed of it all.'

Would she judge someone for a three-month engagement? I ask her.

'Definitely.' We both laugh. 'But maybe these three months are different to usual three months – we've spent so much time together, and we've seen all of each other. And listen, it's not like I'm certain of this because you don't know what life is gonna throw at you. You know, divorce is a reality. Separation is a reality. And I'm under no illusion that that's a possibility. But at this point, I can safely say that my intention is to stay with him for the rest of my life. I want to have children with him. And I think that's also part of the reason why I've gone "Oh, you know, fuck it, I'm gonna follow my heart" and go day by day. I'm always worrying about the future. I'm always worrying about bad things that might happen. And maybe this is a time for me to just go you know what, fuck it. I'm going to follow what my heart's telling me at this point. And that is to become engaged to him. And not give a shit what anyone else thinks. There's bigger things happening than my wedding.'

Florence grew up working class like me – and has moved to London to pursue a writing career. 'It's intellectual snobbery, the idea that more enlightened people would sniff at the women we know from our hometowns getting married.' I always think about how that innate judgemental tendency we've all developed since we decided to try to be cool on social media is born out of a heady mix of insecurity (that everyone is basic at heart) and classism (that you're more intelligent than some person who thinks marriage is the most important thing in her life). This makes the process of 'coming out' as pro-marriage, or as engaged, completely terrifying. Perhaps this means we should get better circles, kinder circles, but wasn't it just a year ago I was at a friend's wedding, rolling my eyes?

After lockdown seeing friends became something different, and their judgements – or perhaps what we let them judge – changed. For my circle, we became hedonistic in an unusually youthful way and our weekly meetings would become spaces where we'd often dance all night by accident, we'd get naked, have a bath together, or just sit up all night and talk and actually actively want to avoid broadcasting the moment online because somehow it felt pointless to do so. There was a pandemic, and a civil rights movement, happening. A shift had occurred, and the daily dross of uploading 'content' to our feeds had begun to feel both boring and irresponsible in a world that had gone through so much pain. Now, a boomerang of Prosecco-glasses clinking felt gauche, to say the least; now, a tbt to a wedding picture felt unthoughtful.

So what happens to love when nobody is looking? Until now, I had never considered the question because people were always looking – or at least I thought they were. But until people stop, or until you're removed from every social situation where people might ask 'how are you and Ace?', their tongues whetted, desperate for you to reveal some terrible dilemma they can help solve so they can feel like a good friend (we all do it, me included), you don't realise that nobody really cares that much what you're doing with your romantic life. People are, rightly so, too concerned with their own.

This process changed the way Ace and I communicated. Instead of saving up minor issues and discussing them with the girlies over a bottle of Whispering Angel and a pack of Marlboro Touch – because we're what? Middle class – Ace and I would discuss things more directly.

Of course, I think this sharing among friends is something totally worthwhile, and, if we learned anything from Ms Bushnell, it's that four perspectives are so often better than one when it comes to the quagmire of relationship difficulties. But it wasn't until half way through lockdown – when Ace and my sex, communication, ability to spend time with each other, and want to understand each other, had literally all improved – that I realised I had often created or maintained dynamics in our relationship just so I could give people something to look at, something to discuss over brunch.

In this improved communication stream, Ace and I uncovered new things about each other that would perhaps not have been discoverable if they weren't given so much airtime: stuff about our sex life, our wants for the future, our favourite flavour from the Crunch Corner yoghurt range: his, thrillingly, is Toffee Hoops. Mine? Vanilla Choco Balls.

And then I'd find myself on a Zoom call, two months later, at a conference about love and someone asked me what I value most in my current relationship and I said – something I'd never said before – 'the privacy'. Indeed the irony that this is chapter nine of a book all about our relationship is not lost on me, but Ace and I had gone from being a couple who moved around each other – and sure, saw each other a lot because we share the same friends and the same bed – to a unit which was working out how to make each other happiest because, a bit like for Florence and her new fiancé, all there was now was us. And we were responsible for each other's happiness in a time where there wasn't much to be found.

'After we cancelled the wedding, which I was gutted about, I was worried that we might have nothing to talk about if we weren't organising the wedding,' Holly told me down the phone, 'but to be honest it was all really reassuring in the end. Because there was absolutely no news, no updates, RSVPs, contact with the venue, the caterer, Dan and I actually returned to a state nearer to the early bit of our relationship where all there was to do was to make each other laugh. Weird that cancelling our wedding – something you literally only imagine you'd do if he like cheated on me or something – was the thing that made me more sure than ever that I want to do it when the time is right. But I feel less rushed now than I did before all this, because this kind of put stuff into perspective and made me realise that it's about love and togetherness and not about rushing to do it so I can say I've done it or feel like I've achieved something and show everyone I have. I'm proud of myself for that.'

Even my wedding-obsessed friends were freed from the shackles of the audience being the centre of their relationships. And, to their surprise, a lot of them were more than happy to postpone. 'Is it about having the audience there to validate your love?' I ask Holly.

'Maybe, but to be honest I feel like I need it less now. Like, in a different way, it will be so wonderful to have everyone gathering together and having a big party, and the wedding – after everything that's happened in the world – doesn't feel like the most important thing about the day any more. So it is about the audience, but it's less about them watching now. It's more about the collective act of us being together.'

Of course, the system clung on to marriage. So much so that in the September of 2020 the UK government announced that they would change UK marriage laws – ones which had been set in stone since the late 1800s. After weddings had been cancelled and postponed, in a panic about the economy and the ailing institution that lies at the core of our deeply Christian, traditionalist society, the government decided to allow weddings to occur legally on beaches, in parks, in backyards and even over Zoom. No longer would couples have to traipse to the registry office and have a separate wedding ceremony where everyone acted out the idea that they were getting married right in front of us, a play within a play. Now, you could send a Zoom link instead of a wedding invite and watch your loved ones legally tie the knot from the comfort of your sanitised home. Funny how the government can change something which strengthens the institution overnight, isn't it?

And there Ace and I were on secret holiday, feeling simultaneously glorious and terrified of what an audience might say if they found out. And there, on the beach, under a white cotton sheet that was blowing in the wind like something from a movie that gays love, I asked Ace what he wanted from his future.

I didn't know what I wanted from mine. I didn't know – after speaking to Candace, to Florence, to Sariya – what a wedding was if there wasn't an audience. And, despite my brain-tingles telling me to make a great gesture, I didn't know if now was the time to put our new mode of post-lockdown communication back into the public domain; and an engagement, on the off-chance Ace might say yes, would thrust it right back into the mouths of the audience that had left the auditorium. Maybe this relationship is just for us.

Ace and I don't talk like this all the time. For a long while, at the beginning of our relationship, I thought that was strange, a failure – that he had commitment issues, or I had insecurities so great that if he didn't tell me exactly what I wanted to hear I would go into a tailspin. And in reality it's not strange, unless you go by the standards of love set out for us by unrealistic quizzes in magazines when we're young – many of which told me I would need a partner who would sit up all night with me discussing my dreams for tomorrow. But so often, as evidenced by

Ms Bradshaw's famous 'can't-live-without-each-other love' monologue, the map is drawn before the love materialises, and when the love doesn't match the map we think it's wrong. Ghosts. But when you're in a long-term relationship so much about the day-to-day of it becomes just that: the day-to-day, the stuff that's not on the map. The what are we having for dinner, and the which episode of this TV show are we on.

I expected love to be big declarations, ineffable emotions, ridiculous gestures. But in reality, love lives so far away from that, that often when those things occur they are there to mask an absence of love. Because, if I've learned anything both through lockdown and through desperately chasing the radical over the normal, it is that so much of life is actually the latter. Even when you're in Corfu in secret on a lounger on the most beautiful beach. It's not big, it's not great, it's very very small.

I expected my love to be something worthy of an audience, a story for the ages, because I always thought the best parts of life were the remarkable parts of life. Perhaps as I'm getting older I'm simply getting more boring, or perhaps – after a life spent chasing the remarkable, the special, the ground-breaking – there's something radical in allowing myself something normal. Something small. Something private. Something that I don't have to sing and dance about.

And that's where this love, with Ace, lives to me: in the small. In the boring. In the mundane. Yes, in the drugs and the sex and the biking around Berlin in dresses that get caught in our spokes, and in the few-and-far-between wild declarations we make to each other. But the real love lives in the moments after those moments – when you come back down to life and it is just quite dull. And you are a person who isn't remarkable – because it's impossible to be remarkable all the time. And real love is there, in the unremarkable, because it's so easy to love someone for being remarkable, while, really, it's remarkable to love someone when they are unremarkable.

It's only through the shedding of this imaginary audience that lockdown took with it, that I saw clearly that there's more love, to me at least, in picking up a pair of socks off the floor and smelling them and knowing that not only they are dirty but they are his dirty and not my dirty. That to me is small, but that to me is also so big in that you know the scent of another person's dirty socks. This intimacy is boring, and yet it's the most thrilling thing I've ever encountered.

'I'd love comfort.' Ace answered, the sound of Grecian waves lapping in the background, as he asked whether I was going to quote him on these pages, to which I smiled wryly. 'I'd love to get to fifty and to feel comfortable in my work and in my life.' Really, this was the first time we'd ever talked about a future that far away.

We, like most couples, make plans for things perhaps as far as a year away – most often, surprise surprise, weddings. Beyond that, the precariousness of being broke queers in our twenties, plus the fear of Actual Commitment, brings with it is something that binds our tongues, and perhaps our hearts too. Even though our actions spell out a committed love, we have both been party to over-promising and under-delivering when it comes to relationships in the past. Perhaps this is something everyone feels, but often it seems like my heterosexual peers find commitment something expected, something guaranteed and relatively easy to make.

It's not that I don't want to be with Ace for the rest of my life – from this view, it's all I can imagine – but as queers we have such a deep knowledge that for us change has been one of the few true constants in all of our lives. It's hard to imagine what is good now won't change in the future. And marriage seems so in opposition to change.

And still, all of this said, as Ace lays out his plans for the future my gut starts to squeeze as it seems decreasingly likely he's going to mention my part in it. We talk about his job, his work, where he'll live, what he'll look like, whether he'll have a dog, and I pretend I'm not wishing he'll say my name somewhere in there.

And then he finished. And I begged with myself not to ask the question. Don't do it. Don't do it. Don – 'and what about me?' – for fucks sake – 'do you see me in that future?'

Ace looked dumbfounded, on the edge of offended but we were in paradise and you can't be offended in paradise. I thought I must have crossed a line, asked for too much commitment, that planning to grow old together is far too saccharine an idea for someone like Ace to get behind, and that I should – after five years – know him better by now.

'Do you even have to ask?' He looked at me, as if to say, duh.

'Well maybe. Kind of. Do you?'

'Of course. That was all chat. The one thing I know for sure is that you'll be there. Don't you know that already?'

Truth is maybe I did. But maybe I didn't. I can't remember whether we'd ever said it to each other, at least not before midday and sober. And I'm certainly the kind of person who likes reminding. 'I'm certainly the kind of person who likes reminding.' I reminded him.

Then he said that he thought all the things we do together, and all the ways we are together, and the ways we annoy each other, and the ways we don't when we really should, are reminder enough. And then I realised how duped I'd been by *Sex and the City* and the monthly quiz in women's mags that I needed to be told that, rather than shown it.

I wonder why this is. Why so many of us find it so hard to read actions above statements. I think of friends who get more angry when you don't text them back than they do if you don't see them for weeks. I think of the fact that I feel a rush when somebody replies to my Instagram story with a fire emoji, but that I can't take a compliment in real life. I think of people who obsess over the statement of love that a wedding brings with it, rather than all of the things that happen before and after it.

I think of how much we've equated love with audiences. How a friend who has never made it to a birthday party of mine for their own reasons got angry at me when I didn't post a birthday message on my Instagram stories, despite the fact I'd sent them twelve (12!) messages of joy and love and celebration the moment I woke up on their birthday. I think about how it feels so much better to sing in front of an audience than for myself. I think about how I love it when Ace rubs my back or holds my hand, albeit very infrequently, in front of our friends more than when he does that in our own bedroom every night. I think about how I want that feeling to change.

Is that all weddings really are? Audiences validating your love? Does doing it in front of people make it more concrete? If wedding-related popular culture has taught us anything, the answer to this is absolutely yes. How many shows and books and films and articles are there about the bridezilla who got so obsessed with the wedding she forgot about the groom? We all remember how humiliated Miss Caroline Marie Bradshaw was when Mr John James

Preston stood her up at the New York Public Library? She dropped her flip-phone, for Pete's sake. And audiences of gals and gays globally intook sharp, painful breaths imagining ourselves being so humiliated that our gorjus bf would be fifteen minutes late for an event so absurd she had a bird on her head. Even she, the most self-involved of all of our television heroines, is aware how absurd the bird was. Although as a sixteen-year-old blossoming fashion fag I can't deny that I adored that little blue bird.

When we talk about weddings we so often talk about doing it in front of those we love, often for those we love. When I think about mine to Ace I almost think it would be a shame to wait until we're forty or fifty and do it for property reasons (let's be honest, it's going to take two decades to save up for a wee one bed in Zone 119,004) because by then it's likely someone very close to us will not be there to bask in our love. Nor will we be able to bask in their love for us. Or in ours for them.

Really, when we boil it down, what is a wedding unless it's to be done in front of an audience? And really, when we boil it down, what is love if not how you are together when there's no audience to watch?

So I keep quiet. I lay back on my sun lounger, and try to think of all the ways Ace shows me he loves me rather than tells me. And I decide not to ask him to marry me there and then. Not because I've reached a conclusion and decided I don't want the wedding, the marriage and the audience. But because this moment together was more full of love than any of those things could be.

Acknowledgements

First of all, thank you for reading this. This book was constructed out of curiosity and a genuine want to ask a question that I couldn't find the answer for. I hope it helped you answer some of yours.

To my parents, who I thank for everything, and in this instance their open-heartedness and their ever-growing acceptance in allowing me to pick things apart. My siblings, too, who have endless patience and are each uniquely inspiring in their approach to convention and the bucking of it. To Grandma. Miss you always.

To my friends, always to my friends, whose ideas are woven into this book, and all my thought processes alike from years of debate, conversation, jokes and all trying to work out how to fit and un-fit into the jigsaw of expectation and normality together. We are very lucky. Thank you all for showing me other ways of being together.

To name names: Hatty, always my first reader – your ideas ignite mine, and I hope mine yours. Wally – Leyah, Jacob, Fran, Margo – for listening to me, and challenging me, every night over dinner while I wrote this book. Long live Wally! To Thurstan, the cake to my peach. Daphne, for still believing in romance. Emily, for still believing in cynicism. Talia, for still believing in marriage. Thank you to Amrou for backing me intellectually. To Amnah for always having the space and time to listen to things that are and aren't to do with work. To Rina for making me cackle and making me think. To Emma for breakfasts and walks and a decade of love. Charlie P, for bat-bat laughs and endless fags. Charlie H for big hair, or no hair, and for Bethan and Matt. Kai, my love for you is huge and my awe for you even bigger. To Allegra, for everything! Everything! (More to come!) To Claudia for being Blunt by name, but not by nature. Travis for being such a supporter! The feeling is more than mutual. To Amelia for such in-depth support and endless cheekiness. Temi, for (many) an important conversation outside a coffee shop. Shon, for the DMs of dreams.

To Celine Dion – the dog and the singer – you both mean the world to me.

Thank you to our wild chosen family. Ellie K, Decca, Harry P, Liam H, David, Eve, Jamie, Matt J, Jessie, Anna, Harriet, Tamara, Max H, Nickie, Howie, Freya, Sam S, Sadhbh, ShayShay, Finn, Otamere. Always.

To my Dolls. Beth, Matt, Hannah, Becky, Amy, Sara, Rach H, Welly. Thank you for offering me a new perspective.

To all of those I interviewed, thank you endlessly for your time and your insights. Your voices made the book come alive, and I was constantly challenged by dipping outside of my small bubble and into other people's worlds.

Thank you in endless waterfalls to my editor, Faiza Khan for acquiring, and believing in, this book. For allowing your ear to be bent, and your stance to be swayed (if only for a second). You have lit up countless days over the past year and a half and I've learned more about marriage from you than you have from me. I adore you! To Allegra (again), for being the smartest, wittiest fountain of both intellectual and pop cultural knowledge. You are everyone's favourite person, rightly! To Lauren Whybrow – thanks for keeping me in check, and some really wonderfully wild emails. And to Saba Ahmed for making the book sing so much better than I could have. Thank you to everyone at Bloomsbury who has had a thought, a hand, a word in here. Bloomsbury, bitch! That's so chic!

Zoe Ross, the most critical, critically engaged, and – critically – generous friend and agent a person could ask for. Kitty Laing, thanks for being here from day dot – I have a feeling you'll like this one! Isaac Storm for all your help, and all your patience. Eleanor Jackson, for repping me in the States and always being so engaged and encouraging. To the team at STV – can't wait to see where this one goes!

Thank you immeasurably to the editors who have empowered me to write over the years. Most especially to Jenna Johnson. My heart flutters when I receive an email from you.

I was so lucky to have such a wealth of worldly knowledge to draw from in my writing of this book. But special thanks Faramerz Dabhoiwala for *The Origins of Sex: A History of the First Sexual Revolution*. It taught me so much. Timothy Wolf's 1985 book *Bisexualities*; *Open Marriage: A New Life Style for Couples* by Nena and George O'Neill, and

Acknowledgements

Janet Hardy and Dossie Easton's *The Ethical Slut: A Guide to Infinite Sexual Possibilities*. Clare Chambers' *Against Marriage: An Egalitarian Defence of the Marriage-Free State* was hugely formative. There are also endless studies and articles that I read in research, which were so useful in their agreement, and disagreement, with thoughts I'd dreamed up. It's nice to know I was not alone in my frustrations or my curiosity.

To the queer community and the drag community. All of this is us. What a privilege it is to be queer, and what a privilege it is to be a part of this community. I hope to always be shown Other Ways To Be Together.

And finally, to Shugs. Thank you for loving me even when I'm writing about the most intimate parts of our internal life. You're a saint, and a wonder. And I would marry you. Or I wouldn't. Maybe. Who knows.

A Note on the Author

Tom Rasmussen is a Northerner based in London. When out of drag, they write for the *Independent*, *i-D*, *Dazed*, *Guardian*, &c. In 2019, they were named one of the hundred most influential young creative voices by the British Fashion Council. Their first book, *Diary of a Drag Queen*, was long-listed for the Polari First Book Prize 2020, and they are currently developing it for screen. They make up half of the pop-punk duo Thigh High, and Tom's debut solo album will be released in late 2021. When in drag, Crystal is a singer but not a dancer. A self-described global phenomenon, Crystal has played everywhere from Glastonbury to an alleyway in Hackney. They have an English Bull Terrier named Celine Dion.

@tomglitter

A Note on the Type

The text of this book is set in Baskerville, a typeface named after John Baskerville of Birmingham (1706–1775). The original punches cut by him still survive. His widow sold them to Beaumarchais, from where they passed through several French foundries to Deberney & Peignot in Paris, before finding their way to Cambridge University Press.

Baskerville was the first of the 'transitional romans' between the softer and rounder calligraphic Old Face and the 'Modern' sharp-tooled Bodoni. It does not look very different to the Old Faces, but the thick and thin strokes are more crisply defined and the serifs on lower-case letters are closer to the horizontal with the stress nearer the vertical. The R in some sizes has the eighteenth-century curled tail, the lower case w has no middle serif and the lower case g has an open tail and a curled ear.